Strength for the
Sandwich Generation

D0068727

Strength for the Sandwich Generation

Help to Thrive While Simultaneously Caring for Our Kids and Our Aging Parents

Kristine Bertini

 PRAEGER

AN IMPRINT OF ABC-CLIO, LLC
Santa Barbara, California • Denver, Colorado • Oxford, England

Library of Congress Cataloging-in-Publication Data

Bertini, Kristine, 1955–
   Strength for the sandwich generation : help to thrive while simultaneously caring for our kids and our aging parents / Kristine Bertini.
       p. cm.
   Includes bibliographical references and index.
   ISBN 978–1–59884–364–4 (hard copy : alk. paper) — ISBN 978–1–59884–365–1 (e-book)
1. Sandwich generation—United States. 2. Middle age—United States—Psychological aspects. 3. Middle-aged persons—Family relationships—United States. 4. Caregivers—United States. I. Title.
HQ1059.5.U5B375   2011
646.7′8—dc22   2011001699

ISBN: 978–1–59884–364–4
EISBN: 978–1–59884–365–1

15 14 13 12 11   1 2 3 4 5

This book is also available on the World Wide Web as an eBook.
Visit www.abc-clio.com for details.

Praeger
An Imprint of ABC-CLIO, LLC

ABC-CLIO, LLC
130 Cremona Drive, P.O. Box 1911
Santa Barbara, California 93116-1911

This book is printed on acid-free paper ∞

Manufactured in the United States of America

For my husband, William J. MacKilligan
There is no one I would rather be sandwiched with . . .

Contents

Acknowledgments

This book could not have been written without the grand presence of my father, George E. Bertini. He is the greatest caregiver of all the ages. I salute you, Dad. I bow to him and all the other kind souls who care for loved ones against all odds and with the deepest love imaginable.

ONE

Introduction: Multigenerational Caregivers

When we think of a sandwich, the best part is what is found in the middle. The filling between two pieces of bread might be rich roast beef, tuna, vegetables, cheese and ham, or any number of main events prepared to delightful perfection. We look forward to what falls between the two slices of bread, and the sandwich is noble for its ease of preparation and ability to be modified to every preference. Yet we do not often spend much time thinking about the sandwich, or the fillings. We take the sandwich for granted. And that is not unlike our failure to appreciate the Sandwich Generation, millions everywhere all around us, caregivers that are a staple in society today, sustaining families and fulfilling so many basic needs, with no fanfare.

Of late, more attention has been given to the phenomenon of the Sandwich Generation: individuals who have come to midlife and find themselves "sandwiched" between their children and their aging parents, nurturing, providing for, and filling what can seem like nonstop, too numerous, and maybe even overwhelming needs of both their offspring and their elders, most often while carrying career demands and household chores, to boot. The Sandwich Generation is the filling, the variable that often keeps the family together, nourished in every way, and running. These individuals come in all shapes and sizes and from differing backgrounds and histories and have varying philosophies. While their differences may be profound in terms of culture, finances, education, and emotional resources, they have many things in common in their role as multigenerational caregiver.

It is significant that more than 50 million Americans are considered to be middle-aged. This number constitutes at least one-fourth of our population. This group of Baby Boomers "earns most of the money, pays the bills and makes many of the decisions. Thus, the power in government, politics, education, religion, science, business, industry, and communication is often wielded not by the young or the old, but by the middle-aged" (p. 231).[1]

During midlife, many people come to terms with their life, and they solidify their self-identity during this developmental period. Traditionally, at midlife, individuals have often found their life partner, may have been divorced, have solidified their professional life, and have had children. Others are less traditional; they may have decided not to wed, have children, or focus in one area of employment, but they also have developed a strong sense of who they are in the world. Still others may enter midlife without having come to terms with their life path, and they may not yet have solidified or embedded their identity.

Erik Erikson, a pioneer in research on the stages in the life cycle, identified the period of midlife as one in which individuals develop either generativity or stagnation. He described the person who has a strong sense of creativity, is successful, and is making a mark on the world with the term "generativity." This person is also concerned with the next generation, and Erikson called the virtue associated with generativity "care." Love is given without expectations of a specific return and is connected to the generations to come. Too much generativity, however, can lead to overextension, which creates unhappiness in that the individual has no time for himself because he is so busy. According to Erikson, individuals who do not develop generativity will experience a sense of stagnation. These people can be self-absorbed, be unconnected to others, and tend to offer little to society. Too much stagnation may lead to a failure to create any sense of meaning, a state that Erikson called "rejectivity."[2]

This book details the challenges one faces at midlife as an individual. It also explores the many challenges of the multigenerational caregiver, who is trying to nurture and care for both children and aging parents. Sandwiched between one's children and one's elders, the midlife individual may reach a healthy generativity or may burn out or stagnate. The challenges at midlife may be huge, so this book offers hope, and a concrete plan of action, for the overwhelmed caregiver.

Much like the traditional sandwich, whose filling is the best part, midlife can be the best part of one's life journey. Midlife is not the beginning, when we are struggling with basic trust, autonomy, competence, and identity issues. Nor is it the end, when we face the impending demise with either wisdom or despair.[3] Midlife and multigenerational caregiving can be that middle place, and as spicy, sweet, or mild as we choose to make them. This book is designed to help the caregiver focus on what is good during what can be a stressful period of life and find joy.

Interestingly, the Sandwich Generation is now officially registered within the National Special Events Registry, which marks a national observance annually each July 1–31. According to the Pew Research Center, just over one of every eight Americans aged 40 to 60 is both raising a child and caring for a parent, in addition to between 7 and 10 million adults who are caring for their aging parents from a long distance. Projections from the U.S. Census Bureau indicate that the number of Americans aged 65 or older will double by 2030, to 70 million. Currently, more than 42 million women fall into the range of the Sandwich Generation.[4]

The tasks of multigenerational care for the midlife individual may seem overwhelming. There can be children of varying ages still in the home—from youngsters to adolescents and even young adults—who make up one side of the sandwich. On the other side, there are aging parents, who come with their own complex set of needs. Many elderly people have physical and mental challenges that they do not have the resources to cope with on their own. Thus, each side of the sandwich needs help from the filling to survive and succeed. The midlife individual, in the middle, attempts to be all things to both sides, children and aging parents, to make the sustenance work. At the same time that the midlife person is managing her own life, relationships, and profession, she may also be attending sports events for her children, helping with homework, making meals, and putting a finger in the dike of the typical daily crises of the children. While doing this, she may also be caring for one or both parents: scheduling and providing transportation to doctors' appointments, attending to the demanding needs of the demented parent, and providing assistance with physical needs that ranges from cutting toenails to dressing, bathing, giving medications, making meals, and feeding.

Americans have come to expect longer lives; thus, more midlife individuals have parents who are still living, and more of these parents are contending with chronic diseases from Alzheimer's and arthritis to cardiac conditions, diabetes, osteoporosis, and hearing or vision loss. In addition, women are deciding to have their children at later ages, so their parents are older at the same time that their children are younger than was the case in years past. Many midlife women are also choosing to adopt; thus, they are parenting into later life. Most women in the Sandwich Generation work outside the home, making it even more challenging to balance both work and the needs of their children and parents.[5]

According to Charles Pierret, up to 33 percent of 45- to 56-year-old women are caring for both their children and their parents. He noted that only a little more than 1 percent of this group has both parents and children living with them, so the care provided to elders often also involves time-consuming travel.[6]

The financial resources used to support and care for both children and elders must also be considered. Monetary outlay can be considerable. Younger children living at home require new clothes, braces, driver's education, and tutoring and need monies for extracurricular activities and a multitude of other routine expenses. As these children get older, college payments loom and are more significant now than ever before, with tuition skyrocketing at the same time more and more careers are demanding degrees. Financial support of an elder may also be significant if the elder has not planned for retirement, for chronic disease care, or for simply living as long as we do today. The midlife caregiver may find himself paying for a parent's groceries, home cleaners, medical care, insurance, prescriptions, home safety devices, and general upkeep. Some elders may require in-home assistance, and if the caregiver is working, this also must come out of the family budget.

Living arrangements for the elderly parent may be in question. Does the adult daughter choose to have the parent(s) come to live with her? How will this impact the dynamic of the primary relationship with her partner and with the children still at home? What about space? There are certainly pros and cons for having the elderly parent come to reside with the family that need consideration.

This book maps out a guide for those at midlife who are struggling with these considerations and more. It offers a plan for sanity while balancing the challenges of being a multigenerational caregiver and gives concrete suggestions on how to nurture oneself while caring for loved ones. It addresses the complexities of caring for parents with whom one may have had a negative life experience, and it explores ways to manage life with a demented parent.

This discussion begins by exploring the tasks at midlife and the psychological impact of reaching the middle of our years. It is crucial that one has in place the foundation for identifying the strengths and weaknesses of the self at midlife before the caretaking of others can be fruitful. Unless the self is wholly recognized and nurtured during the middle years, the assistance to others will be filled with resentment and will be ineffective.

The book reviews the parenting of children during midlife and the special joys and trials that are faced as skinned knees are bandaged, proms are celebrated, and children are launched into young adulthood. Next, the complications of caring for elders are discussed within the context of the family. Relational bonds are examined, forgiveness is addressed, and the creation of a balance between children and parents is explored. Helping all generations of the family to create joint meaning as days dwindle for the elder is also discussed.

Embedded in this work is a chapter that assists the individual at midlife in finding ways to nurture himself and his primary relationships. It spells out a concrete plan that can help him manage each piece of the multigenerational caregiver package during midlife and offers worksheets on which to design one's own individualized plan from the suggestions that are offered.

A discussion of the life cycle in different cultures provides a new lens through which to look at how others in the world care for their children and aging parents. The phenomenon of the need to be loved and cared for permeates all societies and cultures and provides common ground to look at the midlife role. A section is included on meaning at each stage of life and the practice of creating rituals, celebrating, and remembering. This is an important chapter that assists readers in weaving their world and families together throughout the generations.

Finally, national and regional resources are identified as potential sources of help for the multigenerational caregiver.

This author is a midlife caregiver to multiple generations. Some days it seems hard to simply survive. Some days there is a joy that is unimaginable, although this may last for only a brief second until the next task appears. I write this book from a combination of research and my own experiences to assist the many others who are experiencing much of the same exhaustion and delight that I do. My hope is to help others expand the moments of delight so that they overpower the exhaustion and to coach others to give in to the exhaustion when it is needed and care for the self.

Here is my brief story. I am 55 years old, clearly at midlife. I work full-time as the director of busy health and counseling clinics at a midsized university. I am an author. I am married and have young stepdaughters, ages 10 and 11. I have two elderly parents who live in our home with us. My mother is 78 and has Alzheimer's; my father is 82 and is sharp as a tack, but he has been in and out of the hospital with a multitude of illnesses, including a broken hip. Adding to the family constellation are our three Ragdoll cats. So, you see, I understand. While your life story may differ from mine in significant ways, the underlying context of being a caregiver remains consistent between you and me. We are universal in our roles, and creating the most gracious and loving way to be who we are is my heartfelt goal for this book.

I am up in the morning at 5:30; my husband (a saint) does the morning duty with the children and gets them their breakfast and off to school or camp as I head out the door to work. I never leave without seeing them or kissing them good-bye, but I do not have the luxury of sitting at the breakfast table to enjoy the morning with them, which is a great regret of mine. My father and mother rise later on their side of the house, and Dad prepares breakfast for Mom, cuing her to wash up, bathe, and eat. During each day, Dad tries to take Mom out for a ride or visit. My dad is an amazing fellow who has the patience of an angel, as my mother cannot be left alone, experiences paranoia, and must be cued to do any task. Dad tires easily, and Mom does not nap, a common trait of Alzheimer's patients, so it is challenging. Dad refuses home help, as he is proud. I am afraid for him, for them, all the time.

During the day, I call to check in. Work is a blessing; it is my respite. My profession is exciting and rewarding, and the days are full. In the early evening, my workday at the clinic begins to wind down, and I get ready to propel myself home. I am the evening "everything-for-everybody." If I am lucky, I get home before the kids, change into my scruffies, set the din-ner table, and start the meal. Mom wants to help, which doubles the time of any task. She places silverware helter-skelter; stands in the center of the kitchen, her favorite spot, so I have to walk around her; and wants me to look at a picture of her childhood for the 18th time that evening. Dad has gone to the computer room to play solitaire for a bit of respite, very much deserved. I understand his choice in computer games. Within a few minutes, the door crashes open with joyous kids, dirty from the playground and filled with stories of the day, both talking at once and vying for my attention. "Kristine, Kristine, Kristine, Kristine!" How many times can a child say my name in a minute? My husband fumbles in the door behind the kids and looks disheveled and faded from his day. I know I am the one on prime duty. I start the laundry and clean the litter boxes while the dinner cooks, and the kids trail me from room to room, saying "Kristine, Kristine!" My mother also follows and tries to "help." It's about now that I want to hop a plane for the islands. I take a deep breath. We say grace and eat. Dinner is a lovely time; the kids take center stage on the nights they are with us, and my parents enjoy their interactions with them. We share our day, and on special nights, we all have a scratch lottery ticket and share stories about what we would do if we won.

I was once told that doing something that doesn't work over and over again expecting a change is a sign of insanity. Well, by the time dinner is over, I must be insane   because every night the same things happen. After the kids clean their places and go to start their homework, the men sit at the table and talk. Mom "helps" by again standing in the middle of the small kitchen, so I have to continually move around her with dishes, garbage, and glasses. Every night I say (I should just make a recording), "Mom, could you clear the table for me instead of standing in the middle of the room?" And she gets hurt. And I feel badly. And she remains in the middle of the room. And I want to really get on that plane.

I then get my parents' bed ready for nighttime and put out my mother's nightgown. I tell her it's time to get on her nightgown, and every night she says she doesn't have one. So we go and find it—placed out for her, as always, on the bottom of her bed.

Then it's time for the kids' homework and baths. I don't know about you, but if you really want to feel dumb, try doing a 10-year-old's math homework. I have a doctorate and can't figure out their math. In some ways, this gives me a break because then they take the math to their father. Otherwise, we do spelling, English, social studies, and special projects. With luck, no one has a meltdown (including me). During this time, I also fold laundry, make school lunches, check work email, make bedtime snacks, and return necessary phone calls or pay bills. Family games come next: kids' choice. This ritual is a good one, and we all have fun unless someone is overtired and cranky (again, including me). Then I have a scheduled hour with Mom in front of the television while she drinks a glass of cream sherry and I drink three glasses of wine. (Well, give me a break!) By now, it's nine o'clock, and I escort Mom back to her side of the house with Dad. I look at the cats and say, "Sorry, I just can't play tonight." They give me a dirty look.

Back at our side of the house, we all say prayers, and I go to my bedroom and collapse. I don't think I've looked at my husband all night and remind myself to kiss him in the morning. The kids stay up later than I and read or watch television; sometimes they crawl into bed with me, and we talk or read together, but I am usually the first one asleep. I wake up the next morning with Dorie, the stuffed fish from *Finding Nemo* that forgets everything, under my arm.

So you see, I do understand. And I generally love my life. My plan for this book is to create a way for you to love yours, too.

TWO

Midlife Challenges

CASE EXAMPLE: THE BUSY LIFE

She throws herself face down into the hammock and tries to curl up into a ball and become as small as she can. The tissue she grabbed on her way out of the house is soaked and ragged from her tears. She lets herself cry, deep sobbing tears that make her nose run. She can feel the breeze under her bottom from the hammock, and it feels good as she tries to settle into the rhythm of the wind and her sobs.

The house is full. Her husband is in the kitchen, preparing dinner for nine. She had made the week's menu out and posted it on the refrigerator, done the grocery shopping (two full carts, pulling one and pushing the other), set the table, run errands, and made sure the kids were washed for dinner and one child ready to head out to soccer practice as soon as his plate was clean.

The meltdown was inevitable, even welcomed. On her drive home from work, she had known it was coming; it would be just a matter of when and what might set her off. On the front lawn, her in-laws had been sitting with her parents, enjoying each other's company. She had served them iced drinks (she kept thinking that one of them might notice that she was running in and out of the house and say they were all set, but no). Out of the four parents, only one of them could still hear, so there had been a lot of shouting, saying "What?" and repetition. Her father uses a walker and her father-in-law is in a wheelchair, so movement of any sort is a challenge, and it takes time to get anywhere. Both mothers are still spry and maneuver well, but with their aging has come a sense of entitlement, and they do little to be of help except to offer "better" ways to do things. ("Why don't you use a tray for those drinks?") The grandparents are here for "vacation"; it is certainly a lovely time for them, but for their adult children, ages 49 and 52, this vacation is pretty much a living hell. It is not that they do not love their parents. It is certainly not that they do not want to see them and cherish time with them. It is simply a matter of having so much to do with their own busy lives and taking care of their growing children that it is nearly impossible to find a minute to breathe in the best of times.

She tries to find her rational brain as she lies in the hammock. She should be grateful. The grandparents are all still well and healthy enough to live in their own homes that are miles away, giving them space for most of the year. As quickly as she has this thought, her mind moves to what she knows is coming: one of the grandparents will fall or get dementia or need her and her husband more in some way. She feels guilty for worrying about how she and her husband will manage. She lets herself cry some more.

She and her husband have busy workloads, and when they are not at work, they are dedicated to their three children, now all in adolescence. Adolescence comes with its own—how can she say it politely—bright nights and adventure-packed days: driving lessons that terrify her, teenage sexuality to address, curfews to maintain, drugs and alcohol to fear, athletic practices and events, colleges to visit.

And, heaven help them, what about their own time as a couple? Forget about sex—they are too tired. But perhaps time for a cocktail or a movie? Good luck. They pass like ships in the night, wrapped in their own worlds, managing their own midlife anxieties. These anxieties are huge, a combination of physical and psychological factors that affect their relationship and their ways of being in the world.

Back in the hammock, she knows she must get up and help her husband serve the dinner. The older folks need to be escorted to the kitchen and seated, which is its own full-time task, and the kids need to be pulled away from their music, makeup, and homework to gather for dinner. She just wants to stay wrapped up in a ball in the hammock. She knows, or at least thinks, that someone will finally notice she is missing—once they need to have a glass refilled or to ask to use the car or to find the grated cheese for the table. She sighs, wipes her nose on the pieces of tissue that are left, and rolls out of the hammock.

THE PSYCHOLOGICAL IMPACT OF MIDLIFE

Midlife can be defined as a period of reevaluation and transition.[1, 2] During the midlife period in the life cycle, there can be an extended experience of reflection, both on the past and on what is to come of the remaining years in one's life. Looking back, individuals may both count their successes and grieve what was not accomplished. Midlife is not a condensed period of time; in fact, it can last for the two decades between one's forties and sixties. Researchers differ on exactly when midlife begin and ends, but it is generally within this time frame.

The midlife transition is a different phenomenon from a midlife crisis, and this must be clarified. As stated, the transition through midlife can occur over a long period of time. Conversely, a midlife crisis is a discrete event that may occur within the midlife transition and can be a much shorter, albeit more powerful, experience. In fact, depending on the individual and her own life history, a series of shorter midlife crises may occur during the middle years. A crisis, by definition, is a short-term event characterized as emotionally significant that may create instability and may eventually lead to radical change. It is important to note that not all individuals who enter the midlife transition experience a midlife crisis. Some people greet midlife with grace and ease. They are pleased with their life journey and feel satisfied with their relationships and accomplishments. They look forward to their future. "Epidemiological study of psychological distress in adulthood does not suggest that midlife is a time of out-of-the-ordinary distress, for either men or women. Nor do stressors associated in popular lore with the midlife crisis peak in midlife. Career crises and decisions may be more prevalent in early career than in mid-career. Marital disruption is more characteristic of the early years of marriage than of longer-lived marriages of the majority of middle-aged men and women" (p. 88).[3] It is, therefore, important to note that the historical view that all individuals will face a major midlife crisis is not necessarily true.

Many individuals, however, have some experience of misgiving during the midlife span that could constitute a crisis. As the inevitable "look back" and review of early-life experiences occur and plans for the future begin to form, individuals are faced with dreams of what might have been different. Carlo Strenger describes a way of looking at a person's life as that person's "central creation: The existential experience of having created a life that truly expresses a person's sense of individuality can be called the strength of authorship" (p. 250).[4] Many individuals reach midlife and find that they have not accomplished what they would have liked to and that their aspirations were lost in the day-to-day existence of survival. As these persons look forward to the now-limited time ahead of them, they realize that they may never leave the lasting legacy or have the impact on mankind that they had always hoped would emerge from their lives. This can be a devastating realization and one that can lead to an existential crisis of meaning. Careening along with the development of an existential crisis is the very real realization that death is looming. It is no longer something that is decades away; rather, it is something that will certainly and unavoidably occur within the next few decades. For those who have great fears of death and who have avoided thoughts of their own mortality, the consciousness that death will be arriving in relatively short order is a cruel blow to the mind. When faced with the reality that their lifetimes are finite, even those who have led lives rich with accomplishments may experience crisis.

There are some universal aspects to the midlife period and to midlife crises. The simple fact that we all enter midlife makes it a common experience for all human beings. How midlife is navigated by the individual depends on many factors. Some of these factors can include the person's resilience, the ability to find and focus on what is good and positive, the internal ability to cope with major life events, and the existence of external supports. The journey through midlife can distort one's image of oneself and disturb one's equilibrium; if one has solid internal and external resources to fall back on, the transition will be easier. Not all individuals at midlife are lucky enough to have the kind of solid emotional and physical stability that is especially helpful in navigating the tasks of middle adulthood. Complicating this transition can be one's own mental health issues, financial duress or poverty, physical impairments, and other extenuating circumstances. There may also be family dysfunction that can impact an individual's desire to care for elders and the subsequent need to contend with the guilt of this decision. Learned resilience and coping skills may or may not be present in the midlife individual. The psychologically resilient individual will find that the navigation of the middle years is likely to be more easily mastered.

The good news is that resilience and coping skills can be learned, expanded, and used to buffer the winds of change. In Chapter Five, the reader will find a guide for developing resources and coping skills that can be helpful during any challenging time. Chapter Five offers ways to nurture and care for the self when the world around one is exploding with everyone else's needs and one is left to try to manage not only one's own life but also one's family circle.

Individuals reach midlife, with all their accomplishments and missed opportunities, and look forward. They see that there are a few decades ahead to perhaps fulfill what has not been satisfied within them—to complete their canvas. Beyond that, death sits, waiting patiently. Thanatophobia, the fear of dying, is rarely talked about, yet it is a universal phenomenon. At midlife, it is likely that the prospect of one's own death becomes more clearly defined, and with the knowledge that life is finite, a crisis of sorts may occur.

Questions emerge: What is death? Does the individual avoid thoughts of the finality of life? Does he have spiritual beliefs that help to provide comfort? Death looms and can be terrifying. What happens to the being? To the soul? Is there an afterlife? Even if one is not consciously asking oneself these questions, they lurk at the edges of consciousness, seeping in when least expected. Ernest Becker stated that the denial of death is one of the deepest motivations of the human psyche. He believed that human beings fight to suppress thoughts of death and to combat the unconscious knowing that death is a reality for each individual. Therefore, many individuals attempt to create works that will immortalize them and keep some part of themselves surviving this way well into the future.[5] Works of art, writing, mathematics, inventions, and the act of procreation can all present a way for individuals to funnel some of their anxiety about death. The creation of a memorial to the self that will live on after death helps to provide meaning for individuals in their remaining years. Erik Erikson also addressed this phenomenon in his book *Childhood and Society*, in which he wrote that in the middle years of life the individual is faced with the dilemma of generativity versus stagnation. Erikson described a shift created within the person from a preoccupation with the self to a preoccupation with what the self will leave behind for future generations.[6]

At midlife, the individual faces many emotional tasks. She is looking at her past and either what she has accomplished or what she may have missed. At the same time, she is facing forward to the final years and planning for how she wants to spend them. Compounding these tasks, she is also nose to nose with her own fragility and the knowledge that she will not live forever. The daily demands of life continue while the individual attempts to digest her life and design her future years. Caring for children and elders, continuing to meet the needs of the workplace, and managing home and financial issues all swirl around her as she tries to understand her life. Mastering the midlife psychological transition with grace requires courage, strength, and fortitude. And having a good sense of humor can help.

THE PHYSICAL IMPACT OF MIDLIFE

The Centers for Disease Control report that the United States is on the brink of a longevity revolution. "By 2030, the proportion of the U.S. population aged 65 and older will double to about 71 million older adults, or one in every five Americans. The far-reaching implications of the increasing number of older Americans and their growing diversity include unprecedented demands on public health, aging services, and the nation's health-care system."[7]

As Americans age, they are faced with a complex set of both the psychological changes noted previously and the physical manifestations of aging. While poor health is not a condition of aging, there is a natural slowing-down process that becomes evident over time. This slowing down may be manifest in slower bodily reactions to external stimuli and slightly delayed cognitive responses. In today's fast-paced world, where high expectations set for the individual, it can become a matter of survival to keep up the same pace one has always maintained, even though it takes a toll to do so. At home, demands may stay the same or they may multiply as the person at midlife cares for both children and parents. The workplace does not often offer creative ways for employees to manage their aging, competition, and continual demand for output. To make matters worse, as our economy struggles, midlife individuals may find themselves tiring more easily, yet feeling the need to compete with younger workers in increasingly demanding tasks.

While disease can strike at any time, the midlife years present a fertile ground for the development of bodily ailments. Physical constitutions that may once have been perfectly fit without much work or attention now require a whole-hearted conscious review. Stasis sets in, not because of laziness but rather because the body is naturally slowing and more effort is required to keep the same level of healthiness than in the earlier years. In a trick of the gods, as individuals age and tire more easily, they must now work harder to take off pounds, to eat with more wisdom, and to sleep in routine patterns.

Middle age has been noted to be a time of psychological self-reflection and possible crisis. Is this not enough? Apparently, it is not. Midlife is also the time that one must be vigilant about attacking increasing body fat, high blood pressure, and increasing cholesterol. Women and men both are at high risk for heart attack, cancer, and other diseases that may strike without mercy as they are attending to the many other consuming factors of midlife. To make this information potentially bleaker, as physical transformations occur in the body, sexuality is also affected. "Declining hormone levels and changes in neurological and circulatory functioning may lead to sexual problems such as erectile dysfunction or vaginal pain. Half of men ages 50 and older report at least occasional erection problem. . . . And many women contend with issues of vaginal dryness and a lagging libido after they pass menopause."[8]

The information about aging and its effects on the body may create further psychological distress. Some individuals cringe at their upcoming birthdays, wanting to pretend that they are not aging. The reality, of course, is that no matter how much people may want to ignore their aging, their bodies behave in the ways that they have been designed to behave. They age as all things do and become more vulnerable to the environment. Trips to the physician increase as immune systems are compromised, bones become fragile, and backs are thrown out easily. Aches and pains increase. Mammograms, colonoscopies, EKGs, prostate exams, and visits to the chiropractor all become a routine part of life at middle age. Many cancers and other chronic illnesses such blood disease, heart disease, and diabetes can be diagnosed during this period of the life cycle. New prescription eyeglasses are needed, and we need to see the dentist for gum disease. In general, we tire more. It seems to be a grim picture. It seems that when the most physical stamina is needed to keep up with life's tasks, it begins to dwindle.

This picture is not necessarily as bleak as it appears. If one ponders the alternative, which would be to die early rather than to age, all the symptoms and complaints pale in comparison. Aging is a concept that each person needs to process individually and then to proceed in a manner that is the most effective personally. There is not a right way or a wrong way to age. There are ways to age, however, that can be positive rather than negative, even with all the challenges one faces.

How does one begin to embrace the idea that all the frailties that we experience are what make us human? The way one thinks impacts how one reacts to life's events. The thinking brain can create both negative and positive emotions that can propel actions. So the work during any challenging event is to find a way to focus on the positive rather than on everything that is wrong.

The Institute on Aging at the University of Wisconsin published a study of midlife called *Midlife in the U.S. (MIDUS)* in 2002.[9] This study revealed several interesting findings that support our ability to age gracefully during the midlife transition, including the following:

- As people age, it appears that it takes more for them to become upset. This finding is based on the fact that more positive emotions were reported than negative emotions during the middle years.

- As people age, they appear more likely to accept who they are and feel more in charge of their situations and responsibilities. This seems more evident among individuals with more social and financial resources such as college graduates and those with stable occupations.

- Although it is commonly thought that aging impacts cognitive functioning, impairment may not happen until old age—and even then, not to everyone! According to *MIDUS*, middle-aged adults showed little decline in mental speed, reasoning, and short-term memory compared to younger adults. Midlife adults performed better than the elderly in the same areas. What is even more striking is that midlife and elderly adults both outperformed younger adults in vocabulary tests.

• As age and the hip-to-waist ratio increase, more effort is devoted to health, especially by women. As age increases, both men and women reported fewer daily stressors.

Those who are in the midst of midlife have the choice of creating their own self-prophecy. The middle years can be consumed by psychological fears and uncertainty, which may multiply as the physical self begins to slow and show signs of wear. Or, instead, they can be a time of growth, rigor, and self-care. The choice belongs to the individual and the way he thinks about his circumstances. How does one take what seems to be frightening and insurmountable and change it into a matter of excitement and self-determination?

AGING GRACEFULLY: STRENGTHS AND CHALLENGES

Aging is a universal phenomenon. Unless one passes on from this life early, one will join the millions of people who pass though midlife and somehow survive to old age. What differs from person to person is the quality of life during middle age and how the individual manages the many transitions that take place during this period.

Look around you. There is a wealth of information before your eyes and countless personal examples of how people at midlife manage their world. You will see some that are miserable and grumble through each day. These are the people who are unhappy with their lot in life, and as they begin to experience some of the universal midlife phenomena, such as bodily aches and wrinkles, they cower and complain. Others may take the same set of factors and be able to create a plan for how to better manage the aches with rest and to use humor to talk about their "earned" wrinkles. These people will navigate midlife with greater ease because their resilience will create a buffer against the winds of change.

Resilience may be an inborn part of the human psyche or a skill that can be developed.

The human spirit is one of the most resilient and amazing phenomena of our fragile existence. Time and time again, under the most horrific circumstances, evidence shows that some individuals can survive and even thrive. In the lifetime of every person some incident or trial will test the core strength of that person's being. The level of stress that the specific trial will bring is relative. For example, a divorce is always stressful and brings upheaval, even in the best of circumstances. How the parties involved manage the stress can depend on the resilience of the individuals. Early childhood abuse and neglect create a foundation for the individual upon which all other stressors fall. The more resilient the person, the greater her adaptive functioning will be in the world when other negative life stressors befall her. Divorce, illness, tragic accidents, job loss, war, loss of a loved one and a myriad of other tragedies can befall the adult. When these issues are compounded by the early vulnerabilities of abuse, neglect or tragedy, the effects can be potentially catastrophic if the individual is not resilient (p. 36).[10]

Some of the lucky have been born with traits that foster an inner resilience; others have to become aware that life and its travail require a conscious building of skills that can help one to cope in a world that is often filled with uncertainties.

For some, the passage through midlife may be unconscious. Days meld into weeks and then into years, and she arrives at old age without much ado. Perhaps there is something to be said for this unconscious process, which does not create any form of anxiety for the person making the passage. This person, however, has created a life without reflection. This manner of living is not necessarily good or bad, and there actually may be some appeal in passing the days this way.

For others passing through midlife, the unconscious can also play the part of hiding the fears and distress beneath the surface of a well-protected shell. Some of the symptoms of anxiety created by aging may emerge without a clear and thoughtful understanding of the source. Grumbling about the generalized discomforts of midlife can occur on many levels and have varying degrees of impact on the self or others. The buried fears about the larger questions of midlife, such as the fear of dying and the meaning of a life well spent, may never come to the fore for exploration. The symptoms of unhappiness may be present without actual insight into a larger explanation for the distress.

Yet others barge into midlife with straightforward plans to evaluate their life plan and become surprised at the internal upset that is generated by their findings.

While entering and weaving through the middle years is a universal human phenomenon, the way each person manages the transition is based on his own history and has an individual trajectory.

Grace is an interesting concept, often seen and defined through a theological lens. Gracefulness, as defined by Merriam-Webster, is to display grace in form or action; pleasing or attractive in line, proportion, or movement.[11] It may be most challenging to be graceful in form and movement when bodily changes are combined with a greater need for personal output and one is achy, tired, and cranky.

Finding and developing personal resilience is one way for the person at midlife to develop gracefulness, or pleasingness in form and action. To begin this process, the self must first become less unconscious, more aware, and willing to take responsibility and action in turning what could be considered lemons into lemonade. Those who are lucky enough to pass through midlife with little trouble either have skills that are very toned or are very unconscious of that passage. Those in those categories who have read to this point and are puzzled by all the hoopla and turmoil surrounding midlife can shut this book now and pass it on to another midlifer. You are free to pass Go.

For the rest of the midlife troupe, follow along. Becoming more self-aware sounds like an easy concept, but putting self-awareness into action to create a positive outlook can be a great challenge if it has not been learned or practiced through the life cycle. Many of life's coping skills are instilled by caregivers in the formative years. Children who are raised in a home in which they are loved and in which the caregivers have a positive outlook will grow up with greater resiliency skills. They will feel that, even if they make mistakes, they are still cherished, and the world is a place that has much to give them. These individuals will face difficult challenges, as all in life do, but may have an easier time adapting to adversity because they have had hope instilled in them from an early age. Erikson described the first 18 months of life as a time when the child will learn to either trust or mistrust. From this period of life can emerge the basic strengths of drive and hope.[12] That being said, a child who is raised with a hopeful view of the world and the ability to trust will ultimately have an easier time of gracefully passing through life's parade of obstacles. Individuals who have hope and trust in the future believe that they can impact their own destiny and have a greater sense of personal well-being. For less lucky children who are raised in homes in which there is chaos, confusion, and sometimes abuse, the ability to trust and have hope for a shining future can be compromised. These individuals will have to work a bit harder to change the early ingrained messages they were given; change can certainly be accomplished but may require more effort.

The playing field is not equal for those entering midlife. It makes sense to look at the complete life history of individuals to understand why some have more difficulty managing the challenges of their developmental milestones than others do. The foundation that is laid early in life is a key for setting the stage for later life responses.[13]

The individual who has not had a proper foundation laid during the early years can learn ways to adapt. Learned adaptations can occur at any time within the life cycle. These newly learned responses can foster more positive responses within the self and from the environment.

It is true that individuals who have been raised with better early parenting and a more solid foundation can have an easier time at midlife. However, they may also find themselves troubled with both the concrete and the existential questions that naturally arise during this developmental phase. Adaptive functioning weakens under stress, and reminders of previous success using positive cognitions and self-care are crucial.

It appears that almost everyone could use a little help at some point during the middle years. The move through midlife is universal, non-negotiable, and a shared human phenomenon. There are ways to make the journey a more stable experience—even a pleasant one—for the most part.

The ability to shift to a healthier developmental path through midlife depends on how one thinks. For example, imagine two separate drivers facing the following scenario in which they are injured:

> A driver loses control of her car as she drives around a corner during a downpour and hits a telephone pole. The damage to the vehicle is significant, and the driver is badly hurt and taken to the hospital. The driver is in a coma for a brief time and awakens to find that she has lost one of her eyes in the accident and suffered bodily scarring.

Driver 1 is distraught. Her car has been totaled, and she has lost an eye. She fears that her appearance is ruined, and she cannot face her husband and coworkers. She cannot imagine living with only one eye, and as she thinks about her losses, her feelings funnel into grief and despair. As she slowly recovers physically and begins to take stock of her situation, she laments her luck. She has limited savings, and her insurance will not cover the cost of a new vehicle. *Driver 1* does not know how to reach out for help; instead, she isolates. She finds herself avoiding work although she is physically ready to return. She eats more to comfort herself. She finds herself crying uncontrollably and has difficulty sleeping, imagining the accident over and over.

Driver 2 is distraught. She has totaled her car and has lost an eye. She grieves the loss of her perfect vision and talks to her husband and visitors about her loss and about the accident. She asks to speak with the social worker at the hospital as she recovers physically. *Driver 2* is grateful. Almost immediately, she realizes that she could have been killed instantly and that she has been given a second chance at life. She is thankful that her daughter wasn't in the car with her. Although she has limited savings and her insurance will not cover the cost of a new vehicle, she trusts that she will somehow be able to find the transportation she needs. She seeks to be an active part of her recovery and to adapt to the loss of her eye. She requests accommodations at her workplace and finds her coworkers to be supportive and reassuring.

The major difference between *Driver 1* and *Driver 2* is in the way that they think about the accident. *Driver 1* thinks that she will never be the same and that the accident has ruined her life. Her negative thoughts create a spiral of feelings, including despair and hopelessness, that lead her to isolate herself from others in her life who want to help her. *Driver 1* may have learned negative cognitions or thoughts from her early caregivers, or she may have developed them on her own in response to life's difficult circumstances. The negative thoughts, however, do not help her to function in a positive way. They do not change the situation she is in; she will still be blind in one eye and scarred. In fact, her negative thoughts can impede her healing in many ways. As her thoughts create feelings of despair, *Driver 1* isolates herself. Her loved ones and helpers may become frustrated and find themselves moving away from her, creating further isolation. *Driver 1*'s despair and isolation can develop into clinical depression, which may affect her immune system and hinder her physical rehabilitation. The more this woman thinks that she has no control over her life and specific situation, the more she will experience self-destructive feelings. She is caught in a vicious cycle in which her negative thoughts lead her to unhappy feelings and create behaviors such as isolation, which are not helpful for her recovery. Her thinking is powerful and has a great impact on her feelings and behaviors.

Driver 2's recovery is also impacted by her thoughts. This woman is aware of the losses she has experienced, yet she is able to think about these losses in a larger context. She cognitively knows that she could have been killed, or completely blinded, and that her daughter could have been in the accident with her. *Driver 2*'s thoughts are positive and hopeful. They help her to feel blessed even in the context of having lost an eye and having bodily scars. She knows she will survive and return to her former functioning. Her hope propels her to become active in her own recovery and to accept the help that is offered from loved ones and professionals. *Driver 2*'s thoughts also have a powerful impact on her feelings and behaviors, although in a very different manner from *Driver 1*'s.

The lessons learned from examining *Driver 1* and *Driver 2* demonstrate how individuals can take responsibility for their own destiny, regardless of the circumstances. Altering one's thoughts to become more positive can lead to better feelings about oneself and the world, a state of mind that can promote actions that lead to effective change.

Following are several key points regarding the ability of thinking to affect feelings and subsequently behavior:

- Thinking (or cognitions) creates feeling about ourselves or others.
- Positive thinking is apt to create positive feelings and actions.
- Negative thinking is apt to create negative feelings and actions.
- We have control over our thoughts and, thus, can choose to think more positively, thereby changing outcomes to those that are more positive.
- Thinking (or cognitions) also affects our biological responses and well-being.
- Long-standing patterns of negative thinking can be altered.
- Positive thinking leads to happier individuals who feel better about themselves, the world, and their environment; positive thinking generally leads to productive behaviors.

As discussed earlier in this chapter, midlife challenges can be significant for some individuals. Each individual can choose to meet challenges with thoughts of despair or of hope. As the past is examined and accomplishments are found to be few, the self can either rise to address new ways to meet goals or succumb to feelings of hopelessness.

Changing thoughts from negative tendencies may sound simple. However, these cognitions have generally formed over a lifetime, and the internal recordings of negative messages may be strong. Negative thoughts can be automatic, so the first step in altering negative cognitions is to identify that they are there. For example, *Driver 1* probably does not even realize that she has negative thoughts. Perhaps as a child she learned that she could never live up to her parents' expectations, and as a result, she has had poor self-esteem. Her thoughts are filled with doom and gloom, and this affects her feelings and behaviors. The first step *Driver 1* needs to take to make changes is to learn to identify when she has negative thoughts. In the beginning stages of changing her cognitions, *Driver 1* will find that her negative thoughts occur mercilessly and randomly. As she becomes more aware and conscious of her "self-talk," she may find that she is in the middle of a tirade of internal dialogue that is self-debasing before she catches herself. The old recordings and internal tapes of negative self-talk are strong, but they can be altered with conscious effort.

Once *Driver 1* becomes more aware of her negative thoughts, she can then take steps to begin to change the internal dialogue. She must learn to replace the negative messages with internal dialogue that is loving, positive, and gentle. *Driver 1* will most likely not believe the positive messages at first. She will feel like an imposter when she tells herself that she is worthwhile and can be successful in the world. However, the more she replaces the negative thoughts with positive messages, the more the old tapes of negativity will wear down. If *Driver 1* stays vigilant to her negative thoughts, they eventually will be erased, and more positive thoughts will take their place. She must remember that the negative cognitions were a long time in developing and that replacing them will be a process that will occur over time, as well. She must learn to be gentle with herself as she works to change her thoughts, as it will be self-defeating for her to be critical of herself for not changing faster. If *Driver 1* can learn to have a sense of humor about the work of self-improvement, it will be a plus for her internal work.

The steps in changing negative thoughts are as follows:

1. The individual must identify that negative self-talk is occurring and notice that the thoughts are likely automatic. (The individual may find herself in the middle of a long internal conversation that is self-berating; she should be gentle with herself and find humor in the pattern if possible.)
2. Next, the negative self-talk needs to be replaced with a positive message or messages. The individual can develop several short, positive comments for herself that she can use to replace the negative self-talk. The following are examples of universal positive comments to replace negative thoughts:
   • I am fine the way I am.
   • I am good enough.
   • I am lovable.
   • I am worthy.
   • I can be successful.
3. Finally, the individual must "rub in" the positive comment(s) by repeating it throughout the day, even if it is not to replace a negative comment.

During midlife, when challenges present themselves, it is helpful to have positive thoughts to implement in order to master these challenges.

Even if one has spent a lifetime with negative thoughts, making the change to a positive outlook can never come too late. Making this internal change can be the single most important life-improvement tool one may develop, and at midlife, it can mark a turning point for how one will spend the second half of one's existence. Changing negative thoughts to positive ones creates resilience and can lead to aging with grace.

Aging gracefully requires a sense of well-being and satisfaction with oneself. If an individual's internal dialogue is gentle and loving, she will be better equipped to give love to and receive love from others. The individual's midlife journey will be less chaotic, even if challenges exist.

QUESTIONING THE PAST

Midlife is the natural time for individuals to look back and see where they have come from. Carl Jung noted that near age 40 the individual begins to take stock and to look at how his life has developed up to this point. Jung stated that "the critical survey of himself and his fate enables a man to recognize his peculiarities" (p. 193).[14]

It is widely accepted in psychology and the social sciences that during midlife many individuals look back at their lives and do an informal life review. Daniel Levinson noted that during this review some people decide they cannot go on as they have in the past but decide to choose a new path for the future or modify an old one.[15]

As part of their life review, some people go back as far as their childhood and early developmental years to attempt to understand how and why they are the person they have become. This process of self-revelation can be painful for some as they look, for perhaps the first time, at how they were raised. The path of self-discovery can uncover secrets that one may have kept hidden in the unconscious or purposely decided to tuck away in the recesses of memory. Memories of child abuse or neglect can arise during this period that can lend both pain to and insight into one's adult choices. Life review can also bring up forgotten events that may cause regret for how a situation was handled in the past. This regret can serve as a motivator to change and behave differently in the future.

While these memories can be difficult, they also provide a context for understanding and an opportunity to make different choices. Such memories may also provide a catalyst to make amends to someone who has been hurt in the past by an action or to contact an old friend or acquaintance. For many, past life review can be a wonderful opportunity to look at their history and gain insight into their behaviors.

The process of looking back may not be a formal act or decision and can occur with memories that emerge at varying times. The individual may find himself having moments when he recalls an event or situation from the past as he looks at where he is in the present. The memories may be attached to strong feelings, which can be pleasant or distressing. These memories about childhood and earlier years can lead the individual to have feelings of life satisfaction or disenchantment. If the memories create feelings of unhappiness and if the person continues to recount the ways that he has failed, a midlife crisis may ensue. However, the person with memories of failure may also choose to use these past events as a guide to changing future behaviors. Henri Bergson stated, "If there be memory . . . it is with a view of utility. . . . The function of the body is not to store up recollections, but simply to choose . . . the useful memory, that which may complete and illuminate the present situation with a view to ultimate action."[16]

Alfred Adler described memory as the reminders that one carries about of one's own limits and the meaning of one's circumstances. He believed these serve as a story that is repeated to oneself to warn or comfort oneself; to keep one concentrated on one's goal; and to prepare one, by means of past experiences, to meet the future with an already tested style of action. As the individual recalls the past, he may reflect on a more adaptive lifestyle or modify maladaptive attitudes in the present.[17]

Once a person questions his past and its impact on his current functioning, he then faces distinct choices. His first choice is to continue on the path he has been on and to make no further change in his lifestyle, goals, or decision-making patterns. He may be well satisfied with the way his memory serves him and feel proud and fulfilled by his life. He may have some small goals he wants to set or some past matter he wants to resolve, but overall he has determined that his life has been productive and fulfilling and he has no need to make major changes.

The second choice he may make, after having some time to think about his past and look at his accomplishments (or lack thereof), is to significantly change his actions and behaviors. This may involve setting concrete goals and altering the ways in which he has conducted himself previously. For example, at midlife, this man may look at his current relationships and see that he is isolated and alone. He may wake up one day and notice that all his peers have families and friendships and that this is an area he wishes to develop. He may then look back at his past and identify that he has spent most of his early years focused on developing his career at the expense of nurturing his friendships and developing a primary relationship. As a result, he may make the conscious choice to develop goals less related to work and more devoted to pursuing sturdy relationships. Conversely, the woman who has dedicated her life to home and family may at midlife become aware that she feels a need to fulfill her role in a different manner. This woman may seek to return to school or find employment outside the home that is meaningful to her.

As described in an earlier section of this chapter, an individual's cognitions can determine whether she will master the questioning of her past. If she has a positive outlook, she will look at herself with the ability to see opportunity for growth rather than with distress at how her life has been. Looking back and feeling hopeless and dismayed about past behaviors do not make them go away or change the fact that they are there, lingering in the early years of her life. However, she has a choice. She can use the past to defeat her spirit, or she can choose to use her memories to inform, instruct, and lead her to change.

Regrets can be a motivator for behavioral change and corrective action. Janet Landman et al. suggested that acknowledging missed opportunities can permit a plan for the future: "like pain, counterfactual thought about a regrettable past may serve instructional and motivational purposes—telling us that something is wrong and moving us to do something about it."[18]

CASE EXAMPLE: WAKING UP

Carl moves through his life without much thought or effort. He has always been pretty lucky, and his attractive looks help him easily get dates with most women when he decides he wants to have a fling. Carl has a great job as a self-employed contractor, and he has never thought much about wanting to settle down. He moves from one casual relationship to another and does not think about the many hearts that he is breaking along the way. He feels he is pretty clear with the women he meets about not wanting a commitment, so he feels justified in his behaviors.

Carl sails along in his life. He has built a gorgeous home on the river and has a dog that he considers his family. But now that he is 55, Carl is beginning to slowly realize that he is heading into his final years of life and that he is alone. These thoughts about being alone have periodically surfaced over the last decade, but they were intermittent and did not linger or bother him for long. However, at 55, something has changed for Carl. His body is tiring, and he finds he cannot work outdoors for long periods of time in the colder weather. This is a disturbing revelation to Carl, who has never consciously considered that his time on the planet is limited. The slowdown of his body illuminates the fact that time is finite.

Carl wonders what his life is for and what he has done to make a mark on the planet. He finds himself looking back over the years. Carl's parents passed away in a car accident when he was 34, and his inheritance propelled his business. They had been kind and loving with Carl and had always hoped he would give them grandchildren. For the first time, Carl wonders what it would have been like for him to have had children, and he regrets the fact that he disappointed his parents. He knows he cannot make amends to them because they are gone, and he wishes he had told them more often that he loved them and that he appreciated all they did for him.

In the past, Carl did not think much about his day-to-day rituals. As he begins to think more clearly about his life, everything seems to highlight the fact that he is alone. When he went for his annual physical and had to have a colonoscopy because he was over 50, Carl did not have someone he felt comfortable enough to ask to drive him. He now feels dissatisfied with eating dinner alone in front of the news. He finds himself imagining what it might be like to have someone living in his home with him, sharing morning coffee and dinner. Carl begins to look at women differently.

Carl also finds himself thinking more about what his mark on the world will be when he dies. He wants to do some good but has never really thought about it more than to throw a few dollars into the Salvation Army pot during the holidays. He begins to have some difficulty sleeping and regrets that he has not given more to his community.

Carl also feels some fear. These feelings come as a jolt as he realizes that his physical stature is naturally going to deteriorate and that he is someday going to die. He is afraid. He thinks about the old people he has seen on park benches, sitting alone. He also begins to worry about becoming ill and not having anyone who cares about him. Most of his friends are married and have older children headed into college. What has happened to him? How did he become so focused on his job and the challenge of the next beautiful woman that he missed an entire part of life with building a family?

Carl makes a conscious decision to make his life different. He finds himself scanning the newspaper for community volunteer opportunities. He signs up to take the local EMT courses that will allow him to volunteer for the auxiliary fire department. This one step helps Carl to feel that he is finally giving something back to the community. He finds himself feeling less lonely, as he is out evenings with other volunteer firefighters, and his sleep improves. His dog becomes the volunteer firefighters' mascot, and Carl feels like he has an adopted family of real people for the first time since his parents died. He often eats meals at the firehouse and enjoys the camaraderie of his new friends.

Carl's notion of sexuality and romance is taking a fairly dramatic turn, as well. He is not quite sure how to develop more than a sexual relationship with a woman, but he is determined to try. He finds that many women who are single have children, and this is another new consideration for Carl. His dating becomes a new frontier, as Carl consciously stops himself from telling women on the first date that he is not looking for a commitment. He goes onto a dating site and describes himself as "looking for a relationship."

Carl has not ever really thought about what it would be like to settle down, and as the idea takes hold of him, he begins to imagine how it would be to have a family. He meets a few women on the dating site and begins to date one of them consistently. He is surprised to find that he enjoys having the company and that sharing his space with someone is enjoyable.

Carl had spent his early years focused on his career and had never developed the parts of himself that called for achieving the intimacy that would result in a long-term relationship or for leaving behind a legacy to the world. He had focused on himself, and at midlife, as he reviewed his life, he reached the concrete decision to make changes. For Carl, the changes included giving back to the community (legacy) and developing a significant relationship with another (intimacy). As Carl propels himself down these new paths, his life is taking on deeper meaning and satisfaction.

FACING THE FUTURE

As those at midlife face their future years, they can choose to move forward with a will to make the changes necessary for them to feel more fulfilled, leave a legacy, and adjust to the idea that their lives are finite.

To feel more fulfilled, the individual must first identify the undeveloped parts of herself that she would like to cultivate and acknowledge regrets that she has for the past. Realizing that there are pieces missing in her development and that she may have missed opportunities is instrumental in implementing change. Looking back helps her to assess the present and further determine how she would like her future to look. Re-creating oneself can be an exciting endeavor. It can be a time to make amends for past harms and build a new way of being in the world. While it may take some courage to begin down the path of building a new persona at midlife, the benefits felt in personal well-being far outweigh the cost of staying the same.

The legacy one leaves behind can take many forms and shapes. Carlo Strenger and Arie Ruttenberg referred to the creation of a legacy as having a sense of authorship of one's life; they believed that one can envision one's entire life as one's central creation and individuality. This sense of authorship over one's life reflects the feeling that one has made a mark on the planet and is leaving something behind for others.[19]

It makes sense to infer that at midlife there may be more urgency on the part of individuals to create a legacy, as they are feeling the reality of death. While some may feel the need to create something aside from the self, many philosophers note that one's own life itself can be considered a creation.

The phenomenon of legacy is a delightful idea. It is a concept that the individual can define on her own terms and embellish as she wishes. As noted previously, the life of the individual can be the legacy itself. The legacy that someone leaves may be found in how she behaved during her existence. She may have donated time or money to the local animal shelter, and this could be the legacy she has left. She may have been a kindhearted soul, and this could be her legacy. She may have been a volunteer, or she could be a person who designed a new concept in the workplace. Legacy is personal. At midlife, what can happen for the individual is that she may become aware for the first time that she wants to leave her mark behind. Of course, some legacies can be negative, harmful, or evil. However, if life review occurs during the middle years, old legacies can be replaced with new and life-generating ways of being that will be left behind for future generations.

Other legacies are manifested in works of writing such as personal journals and authorship, as well as in art, music, childbearing, painting, and craft work. Legacy is created through the personal meaning of the individual. The conscious creation of a legacy is an opportunity for the self to provide a symbolic culmination of one's life to those who follow.

It is important that readers do not feel that they need to paint a masterpiece or invent a new gadget to leave a legacy. Legacy can be tangible, but it can also take the form of remembered tenderness, kindnesses, or humor. Legacy can be as simple as remembered bedtime rituals that get re-created through the years for generations.

It would seem that the concepts of reviewing one's life and feeling more fulfilled, of building legacy, and, finally, of coming to terms with death are all intertwined. At midlife, each of us becomes aware that we have a finite number of years ahead of us; this naturally creates a "looking-back" period, which in turn leads to midlife shifts and the creation of legacy. Persons who are aware of the process that is being navigated will likely have greater success in coming to terms with mortality. On the other hand, individuals who remain unconscious of their life cycle may also unconsciously act out their fears of dying and their regrets.

Death is inevitable. Yes, that means you, too. Does the idea of dying terrify you? It is hard to accept that our lives will end and that no matter what our beliefs are, we do not really know what will come next. Will the lights just go out? Will there be a heaven? Will we return to live another life until we get it right?

How can we become more comfortable with the "unknowing" of death? Where do we find comfort? Interestingly enough, if the individual can come to terms with the fear of death, he will have conquered fear of all things. The fear of dying underlies and cushions all other fears. Remarkably, if people dissect their lives and truly look at how they live, they will find that they die thousands of times each day. When you get up each morning, it is the very last time you will ever get up that same way on that same day. This is a small death. When you drank your cup of coffee at breakfast yesterday, it was the very last cup of coffee you would ever have on that morning. Each kiss, every time, is the last kiss in that moment. To take this further, each moment is the very last, never to be experienced again. The understanding and acceptance of death can be a profound experience. Once it is learned and accepted, each small action or event becomes important. Small things are taken less for granted. Words are spoken with a new voice. We become aware of the importance of the moment, and we begin to live like every moment could be our last—because it is.

Death is a wonderful instructor. It can teach us to take advantage of the moment: to say and do what needs to be said and done right then, so there will be no further regrets; to act like there will never be a tomorrow because, for all we know, there may not be one. To fear death less is to embrace life more—to raise one's eyes to the sky and to take in the minute-by-minute beauty and grace that are everywhere. And if the fear is too much and paralyzes us and keeps us from seeing the beauty and grace, then it is time to seek guidance. Guidance can be found in spirituality, in counseling, and in family and friends. Each of us struggles with coming to terms with death; this is another universal tenet.

Midlife challenges are many. The midlife person is busy with work and family. When she thinks she cannot manage one more thing, she begins to become aware of her physical limitations and of psychological factors that create questions and, at times, a midlife crisis. Each person faces midlife with her own set of strengths and personal challenges; if she can learn to master her negative thinking, the path through midlife will become one that can be fruitful. And, finally, as if all this confusion were not enough, there is death! Boldly looming on the horizon, it is the greatest challenge of all. How each individual defines the face of death will help to define the rest of the life journey. Is the face of death kind and loving? Is it horrifying? Is it filled with regret and unresolved issues?

You are the master of your fate. Your life will provide twists and turns, good times and troubled times, ease and hard labor. Midlife provides you an opportunity to reflect upon what is past and to challenge the present with new behaviors that will mark your future. Your conscious self at midlife can create a new and more fulfilled existence. This self can design a legacy for future generations in the simple act of being. Emerging from all the midlife daily bustle, confusion, and fear can be something extraordinary—a new and better version of you.

THREE

Our Children

It is now not enough to be able to balance work, laundry, family emotional bruises, dinner, and the "new math" homework that changes every year. Midlife parents have to learn to grasp developing technology, like operating the Wii and downloading a computer program for school assignments. The mastery of those little rectangular boxes that kids carry everywhere and use to communicate with their friends eludes most of the midlife generation. Adults in their forties, fifties, and sixties were raised with telephone calls, which their parents could overhear, and home visits from neighborhood kids. The process of text messaging and Facebook usage is as foreign to this generation as the horse and buggy were to Baby Boomers.

Madeline is a Boomer. She is a 50-year-old single woman with two adopted children from Cambodia. She has a middle-management position in a small corporation and is able to be flexible with her work schedule. Her children are ages 12 and 14, both boys. Madeline's life has been a flurry of activity since she brought them home from Cambodia. Madeline's mother also lives with her, and this, at times, is both a blessing and a curse.

As "tweens," the boys are active in soccer, baseball, and after-school projects and are interested in girls. Madeline has a van that she feels is more of a taxi and grocery transporter than any vehicle of her own. There are fast-food wrappers shoved under the seats and a variety of sports paraphernalia piled in the rear. The van smells like french fries, and the last time she got into her seat without looking, she sat on a sharp object that she later determined was a piece of a video game. Madeline sometimes fantasizes about owning a small four-door sedan in which she could play her classical music or oldies and simply drive quietly to work.

The boys are awesome kids, but, like all tweens, they are active and self-absorbed. They love their mother, but, realistically, they do see her as the end to many of their needs. As young children, they were also busy and active, but because of their younger age, they were more apt to have time for Madeline. As little boys, they needed her for more than transportation and lunch money and filled her up with the cuddling and affection that older children feel embarrassed to show to their parent. Madeline misses the overt, responsive "little boys" they once were and tries to adapt to the new young men in her life. In some ways, she has to do less for them, as they can manage to dress themselves and most days remember to bathe, but in other ways, their needs are more consuming, and they are met pretty much without thanks.

Madeline now has to buy the specific new jeans of the particular month and worry about drugs and sex. Both her boys are gregarious and popular, and while she is grateful that they do not have social problems, she also worries about her older son getting someone pregnant and her younger son being addicted to the Internet. Madeline is not technologically sophisticated, and she feels like she cannot keep up with the mechanical whoozie-whatsits that her sons are using to communicate with their peers. She worries about pornography on the computer but has no idea how to go online to see what sites her boys have been using.

Many days Madeline feels disoriented, like she is an alien. She is moving so fast through her day that she must consciously stop herself to check if she is still breathing. And in the midst of all her activity, if she slows herself down just enough, she can taste a bit of the love and joy that is buried in the day's chaos.

In dissecting Madeline's day, we can begin to see how slowing down and "tasting the moment" can improve her lifestyle and well-being, even when she is overwhelmed by daily chores. Madeline begins her day at 5:30, when her alarm goes off and she gets up. There are mornings that making her bed feels like it is just too much to do, so sometimes she closes her door and leaves the sheets to "air out." She does not ever allow her sons to leave their beds unmade because she knows that, if she lets slide her boundaries with them, she will never get them back. She has decided that it is her prerogative some mornings to have a messy room. Now she proceeds with waking her sons and starting breakfast. She had set the coffee timer the evening before and enters her kitchen to the most delicious aroma of coffee beans; she breathes deeply and takes a moment to absorb the smell and the first taste of coffee on her lips. As a parent, she has developed her planning skills over the years, so lunches were made the night before, and she can focus on breakfast. Madeline knows better than to ask what the boys would like to eat; she quickly makes the decision for all of them and sets out fruit and begins to warm bagels. She multitasks as she puts breakfast together by using the downstairs bathroom to quickly shower, put on the outfit she laid out the previous night, and put on her makeup. As the bagels pop up, she turns to her counter laptop and checks her work email, the only computer skill she has mastered.

Madeline's younger son is always the first one downstairs, and, half asleep, he plops himself at the kitchen table and downs a large glass of milk. By the time her second son emerges from upstairs, she is sitting at the table; the three have 15 minutes together to eat and talk before the day begins. Madeline's mother sleeps in until later in the morning and will do the two loads of laundry that have gathered in the last 24 hours. Madeline is grateful for this; she wonders how she could manage without her mother's help with these tasks.

Madeline takes another moment to look deeply at her sons and feels the pride she always does when there is a quiet moment. They are handsome, bright, and kind young men, and she reaches across the table to ruffle her older son's hair.

After their brief, quiet breakfast, Madeline launches into the day's litany of drop-offs and pickups, sports events, and dinner plans. Today she will eat her lunch during work, pick up her older son at 3:00 P.M., and take him to a game in the next county. She will not be able to watch his game today because she has to travel back to work for another hour. Her younger son will take the bus home after his guitar lesson, and Madeline will dash home, set the table, throw the chicken in the oven, and then go back to the next county to watch the last of her older son's game and bring him home. Madeline's mother will watch the chicken and prepare the side dishes so that once everyone is home, dinner will be on the table by 7:00.

Madeline wonders if the only time she gets to really see and speak with her sons anymore is at the table. She asks her older boy about his girlfriend, and he does not want to share much, so she decides she will catch him later for some private conversation about birth control. Madeline knows that she alone has the sole responsibility for teaching and helping this young person to grow and develop. She sees this as a joyful experience and wishes only that she had the time to impart her wisdom to him more fully and carefully. She feels like she has to snatch minutes between sports, his text messaging, and his brother. She takes another of those deep breaths and reminds herself how lucky she is to have the opportunity to mold her children in positive ways.

After dinner, the boys help with the dishes while Madeline gets into her bathrobe and the old, comfortable slippers she loves. She washes the makeup off her face and sets out her clothes for the morning. She prepares the coffee, so she will have the pleasure of its smell when she gets up in the morning. She knows she still has several tasks left before she can get into bed with her book. Madeline struggles with helping her younger son with his homework and then, as usual, finally has to call his older brother for guidance. The math is simply impossible for her. She takes her moment when the homework is complete to have a conversation with her older son about sex. He is a bit indifferent, reminding her that they have already had this conversation. Madeline knows she has to let go and trust, which is no small thing.

As nighttime falls, the boys, predictably, use their electronics to communicate with the outside world, which has grown much larger and wider than when Madeline was a teenager. Madeline uses some of the few hours left in the day to spend her obligatory hour or so in front of the television with her mother. Sometimes they play cards, but Madeline prefers TV because she can pay bills or skim the newspaper at the same time. Madeline feels that no one gets enough of her, that she dribbles herself out in drabs to her family because she has not got enough for all of them. She feels guilty about her mother, who is alone all day. She feels guilty that she does not understand the new math or the computer system and that she cannot join her boys at all their outdoor activities. She feels bad when she tells her mother that she is going to bed, knowing that her mother will sit up late, alone, watching television.

In fact, Madeline is usually the first in the family to retreat to her bedroom. Her sanctuary is filled with books, an old-fashioned landline telephone, and a small sitting area with its own small television, which she seldom watches. Her boys come up at 11:00 P.M. and are pretty good about putting lights out on time. Sometimes Madeline misses reading to them and having them fall asleep with her, but mostly she is grateful for the last quiet hour of the night that is hers alone.

Madeline closes the door to her room and delights in her choices. She can call one of her friends or the man she has been seeing periodically. She can read. She can simply sit in bed and stare at the wall, or she can fall asleep.

On a bad night, Madeline wonders what her life is all for, why she repeats the same routines, and what meaning her life has, and she feels lonely and frustrated at never having enough time for herself or anyone else. On a good night, Madeline reviews the things for which she is thankful; for example, she might recall something one of her boys did or said that was extraordinary and feel the satisfaction of being a single mother who can carry it all.

Madeline, luckily, has the good sense and resilience to know that how she *thinks* about her life will affect how she *feels* and that her feelings will ultimately affect her behaviors. When she catches herself going down the path of misery, she cognitively understands that these thoughts will not change things or make her life easier. Most times she catches the negative thoughts and consciously makes herself shift them to the positive. Madeline is also wise enough to know that there are times when it is just fine for her to have a pity party, weep, and allow herself to wallow in misery.

Madeline makes the conscious choice about her thinking and feelings several times every day. She can choose to take deep breaths and recognize and enjoy the moments that are good, or she can choose to focus only on what makes her miserable. This conscious choice of thoughts, feelings, and behaviors is what gives Madeline's life its form and quality. Madeline chooses to greet her days with joy, so she finds happiness even amid the daily chaos.

THE TRIALS AND JOYS OF PARENTING AT MIDLIFE

The trials of parenting can be compounded when caring for elderly parents, as parents are caught between wanting to meet all their children's needs and having to balance the needs of their parents. The numerical ages of the children at home are not especially consequential, as children at all developmental stages require certain parenting skills. Younger children need more hands-on care from their parents, and teenagers demand more independence, yet still need supervision and guidance that they do not necessarily appreciate. At every age, children require attention and love to grow and thrive. From their parents, they need time, which is sometimes the most difficult need of all to meet.

Parenting is a time-consuming endeavor. There are universal needs that children have at all stages of development that parents must fulfill as part of the daily routine. Preparing breakfast, bagging lunches, and creating healthy dinners form the routine in which the family rotates. School conferences, extracurricular activities, doctors' visits, dental appointments, clothes shopping, and bedtime rituals are all universal tasks that parents must somehow find the time to accomplish. As parents try to manage their own work schedules and provide for their children, these multiple demands can compromise the quality of the time that they spend with their children.

Compounding the universal needs of children at every age are additional unique needs that appear at each stage of their development, which create numerous other responsibilities that parents must navigate. For example, when children are younger, they require more hands-on care and supervision. At younger ages, children cannot understand the parents' need to be away or distracted, as they want the world to revolve around them. Young children will find ways to get their parents' attention and will resort to acting out if their needs are not met. While older children do not have the same kind of direct-care needs, they come with their own set of time-consuming issues, such as transportation to and from events, supervision with peers, and complications in their social development as they become sexual beings.

Many midlife parents have chosen to adopt in their forties and fifties, and this subset of parents has its own issues to manage along with all the developmental tasks already noted. These adoptive parents provide a magnified view of both the joys and the trials of being a midlife parent. The joy of adoption is intense. The adopted child has likely been awaited with extreme anticipation and happiness, yet the process of adoption can be a trial. There is considerable paperwork to manage, the search for the child, and issues relating to the availability of the child who is being adopted. Many adopted children come from countries where adoptions can fall through at the last minute, leaving the potential parent bereft. Once the child is safely at home with her new parents, she may have unique physical or psychological needs. The cultural identity of the child may impact the family in ways that were not expected. The tremendous joy of adoption, similar to any parenting endeavor, is laced with trials that are unique to the child and the environment.

Those who adopt as older parents during midlife will be raising their children while they face many midlife challenges. Their "peer group" of other parents at school, at social functions, and at church may be much younger than they are. Parents who are older may feel isolated and involved with a peer group that is developmentally different. Younger parents who have started their families in their twenties and thirties may not be able to relate to older midlife parents. This lack of connection can be a disappointment for midlife parents and leave them without a solid support group to assist them in dealing with parenting issues. It can also be an issue that midlife parents tire more easily and look older. Their children may be embarrassed by their gray hair and note the difference in their friends' parents, who are younger and more active.

While these parents attend to their children, they are also facing the impact of midlife and managing the midlife issues discussed in Chapter One—specifically, their own life review and planning for the future. The decisions they make as they review their lives and consider what changes they may want to make in the coming years will be impacted by their children. They are also generally more tired than younger parents, yet still have to manage all the functions and the needs of their children. Their bodies may not be as capable of playing sports with their children. They also may be much further from understanding their child's school academics, such as new math, than younger parents, who have more recently attended classes.

In addition to these trials, there are special situations that can accompany children that make parenting even more challenging. Children are complex, and many may have unique considerations. Both biological and adoptive children can have physical or emotional issues that require medical attention. There are also circumstances that can impact the family, such as a catastrophic car accident or lingering illness. Each special or unique need will require dedication from the parent as the family members navigate their environment.

While some of these issues may sound bleak, being an older parent has many positives. Children who are raised by midlife parents have the good luck to be able to develop in a home in which the parents are mature and experienced with life. While their parents may not be as quick out of the gate as some of their friends' parents, they often have a great deal more wisdom, patience, and stability than younger parents. These midlife people have generally established themselves in the workforce and are more financially stable than younger people, who are just beginning their careers. Those who parent at midlife, such as adoptive parents, have made a clear choice to raise a child and embrace the idea of being a parent. Younger parents may also embrace parenthood; however, they may not have an experienced and realistic picture of the travails that life can unexpectedly throw at a family. Midlife parents will have experienced many more ups and downs in the life cycle and enter parenthood with a clear lens. They may more fully understand the responsibilities that parenting brings and may have planned for the trials that will certainly arise during the upcoming years.

Older parents have a wider worldview simply because they are older and will have experienced more than younger parents. As they are in the midlife period and "looking back" at their lives, they may try to keep and use many of the more positive parenting skills that they learned from their own parents. These midlifers are more likely to consciously attempt to discard the less loving and more hurtful interactions they experienced from their own parents. The life review that is done at midlife can help to make better parents who are becoming conscious of their own development and what worked well for them as children.

There are both joys and trials in parenting at midlife. While the challenges may be real, the joys are equally powerful. As with any situation in life, if the focus is put on what is positive and good, the difficult aspects will naturally diminish. Trials come with any important work, and having children is the most important endeavor anyone can undertake. Therefore, it would be expected there would be trials in midlife parenting. However, the joys can outshine the trials. Focusing on the good and feeling the love will help the challenges melt away to a small and manageable size. Taking small steps, breathing, and seeing challenges as opportunities while using positive self-talk will light the path to a being a better midlife parent.

SKINNED KNEES, HOMEWORK, PROMS, AND COLLEGE

Children are amazingly resilient creatures. They can thrive when their parenting is "good enough." Donald Winnicott developed the concept of good enough parenting, which is parenting that provides what the child needs to function well in the world. According to this concept, a good enough parent is one who is available to the child and supports the child emotionally through the times that are rocky. The child comes to expect that the parent will be there for him and, therefore, can unconsciously take risks toward independence under the parent's watchful eye. The good enough parent's generally warm and loving attitudes remain in place even when the parent experiences annoyance or anger. While the parent may make mistakes, a fundamentally accepting attitude toward the child overrides any temporary irritation. Good enough parents are able to handle their negative reactions in a constructive fashion, which then helps to create thriving children.[1] During their children's lifespan, parents are "confronted with a fundamental but often difficult task: teaching children the values and regulations necessary to function effectively in society while also nurturing the children's drive to express themselves and to pursue their unique interests and capabilities" (p. 198).[2]

To be a good enough parent at midlife, one must teach one's children values and behaviors that help them, as they grow to function effectively in the world. Midlife parents have had decades to develop their own set of morals, ethics, and behaviors. One of the great benefits of aging is the life lessons that one learns. This knowledge and wisdom can be imparted to the developing child, not by lecture, but through actions and parenting skills. Younger parents simply do not have the years of experience that can increase life skills and knowledge. This is certainly not to say that younger parents cannot be competent parents. Many young parents provide wonderful, loving homes in which their children thrive. By design, however, younger parents do not have the years of life experience possessed by older caregivers that can contribute to a stable, mature way of raising children.

The implications of parenthood during midlife have received relatively little attention in the literature from researchers.[3] However, studies have shown that satisfying parent-child relationships overall were associated with high levels of the parents' psychological well-being.[4] Each adult developmental stage comes with its own set of challenges and rewards; younger parents may struggle financially as they adapt to a new marriage, while older parents may be managing all the midlife issues discussed in the first chapter. The resilience of the individual at any age and the individual's psychological stability will create the foundation within which the child is raised. The more stable and resilient the adult, the better adapted the child.

While the literature may not specifically address the implications of parenting during midlife, there are certainly salient ways in which a midlife parent differs from a younger parent.

It is a fact that children of midlife parents have to manage some difficult aspects of having older parents. Their parents may look different from the other parents; their hair may be graying, and they may not have the energy that younger parents have to play sports and stay up late. Midlife parents may not understand new math and how to use current technology with the same sophistication as younger parents. Children with midlife parents may worry more about the mortality of their parents and fear that mom or dad will die while they are still too young to care for themselves. They may feel embarrassed by the different way that their parents look and what they consider to be old-fashioned thinking compared to their peers' parents. During the early years, children tend to want to blend in and conform with their peers, and having parents who may look more like their friends' grandparents than their parents can be hard for kids.

However, children of midlife parents will reap several benefits that may come with having a parent in the middle years. As discussed, the midlife parent has a wealth of life experiences from which to draw on in parenting. To some extent, midlife parents will likely have begun the life review discussed in Chapter One and may be implementing the changes that they want to make in their behaviors for the next phase of their lives. This life review will benefit the children being raised, as the parents will be much more aware of the long-term impact of their current behaviors on the family. Midlife parents may be working to improve themselves and their other adult relationships, and the positive benefits of these changes will also spill into how they parent.

Because of their life experiences, midlife parents can be skilled at navigating systems such as schools, doctors' offices, and other community agencies to access services for their children. Individuals at midlife likely will have learned to be assertive in speaking up for what they need and less fearful of authority figures; this will be helpful in advocating for their children when necessary. Midlife adults may navigate systems with grace and experience and be much more aware of when it is important to speak up, hold back, or make a demand. They will be less likely to put up with nonsense and may find themselves to be older and wiser than many of their children's teachers and other community leaders.

Midlife and midcareer tend to go hand in hand, and this combination can create a stable financial picture for children being raised by midlife parents. These parents may have been at work in the same place for several years, and their occupations can be second nature to them. The limits on their job stress will promote healthier lives in general, as midlifers are less likely to be concerned about performance or career choice. With a stable employment picture, midlife parents can focus more on their children and the needs that arise at home. The job is secondary; the family comes first.

Personal relationships at midlife tend to be stable. Although some divorces do occur during this period, many relationships become solidified, and partners come to know and understand each other well. Children who are raised by midlife parents who are committed to each other will likely feel the emotional attachment of their parents and understand that they have a solid foundation of family from which to launch. This stable foundation can be the most important circumstance of a child's life.

The response that a young child receives from her parents for a skinned knee can provide a generalized example of how the parents will likely respond to other childhood calamities, both large and small. Nurturing parents, at any age, will promote a feeling of safety for the child, who will grow up feeling secure. Many adults are naturally able to nurture and provide a positive environment in which children can grow. Other adults may not have been raised in homes where they were unconditionally loved, and the ability to nurture may be compromised or undeveloped. In this matter of nurturing, older parents have the luxury of having had a longer lifespan in which to develop and practice the skills of love and consistency. Often, younger parents may not have had time to develop both the emotional and the cognitive skills that mature in individuals through the lifespan. Midlife parents likely will have read parenting books or taken classes to prepare for their role as parents; they will have watched their peers parent and will have made thoughtful decisions regarding how they want to manage their child's developmental milestones. Younger parents may find themselves flying more by the seat of their pants; while they may have done some reading and preparation for their child's milestones, they will not have the life experience that comes with being a midlife parent. Those who refute this concept may argue that younger parents have new and fresh ideas about parenting and may be less set in their ways; this may be true of some younger parents. However, it is also true that with age come experience and a greater wealth of personal awareness and confidence from which to draw one's actions and skills.

The young child with the skinned knee may not be badly hurt but will need consolation and attention from her parent. The instinct of the good enough parent, whether a young or a midlife parent, will be to reach out and comfort the child. This nurturing parent will take the child upon his knee and place a bandage on a tiny mark that may indeed be inconsequential. The act of responding with love is what matters, and parents of any age who are attentive and caring will provide this kind of solace to the crying child. Midlife parents will have an understanding and knowledge from a full life that their child needs the comfort of their arms. This midlife parent, who can now see the finite limit to her time on the planet, may provide parenting with an eye to making the universe a better place through her child. The parent who is progressing in years knows in a clearer, more personal way that time is limited and each moment must be cherished. As the midlife parent feels her own limitations and interacts with her child, the need to make each moment last is palpable.

It is clear in the literature that negative early parenting increases the risk that children will develop adjustment problems.[5] Young parents who come from strong, healthy family environments themselves will likely provide solid homes and good enough parenting to their children. Midlife parents who have both the strong, healthy context of their own upbringing and the life experiences that lead to skill development over time will also likely provide good enough parenting to their children. These midlife parents have the additional benefit of a larger life context through experience, learning, and remedying past mistakes.

As the child develops, he will graduate from the early years and their universal traumas, such as skinned knees, to new hurdles, such as mastering challenging educational concepts and social dilemmas. The reader may recall Madeline's travails with her son's math homework. As a midlife mother, Madeline found herself decades away from school herself and not at all familiar with the new trends in math that her son brought home from school. Younger parents may find themselves more familiar with the educational trends their children experience and academically may be more helpful with their children's studies. However, once again midlife parents have greater world experience to fall back upon. These parents may be more skilled in asking for help from others to catch up with learning. Midlife parents may have more patience and developed skills, which can be helpful to their children in problem solving creatively. Certainly, mature parents will have greater experience regarding social situations such as dating and sexuality. Parents at midlife will have the assertiveness and knowledge to be able to talk with their children directly about these issues. Speaking with one's child about sexuality can be terrifying for a parent, and this nervousness can be picked up by the child. Everyone ends up feeling uncomfortable as the parent attempts to have "the discussion." By midlife, parents will have had an opportunity to develop a level of comfort with their own sexuality and their bodies, and this comfort will be transmitted to their children. The more matter-of-fact parents can be regarding matters of sexual and social growth, the more easily conversations will flow with their children. From skinned knees to kissing to sex, a context of calm understanding and love will help children to hear and feel supported as they develop.

Children begin to grow into young adulthood with milestones that mark their passages, such as driver's licenses, high school graduations, and proms. Parents are faced with a whole new set of anxieties and their own excitement as their children grow up. The letting-go process for parents begins during high school, when their children are spending more unsupervised time out in the world. Teenagers will push boundaries as they seek to master their need for independence, and good enough parents will set limits that both allow them to grow and yet remain within a safety net. This balance is sometimes difficult to achieve; it can take wisdom and understanding on the part of the parents to know when to hold on and when to let go.

The senior prom can magnify the significance of the young adult years. Teens will likely want to go with a date and stay out all night to celebrate. Their parents will worry about alcohol, sex, and drugs. This prom is generally the launching pad to graduation and then college, and parents become aware that their children have grown up and will soon be moving into an independent life. How the parent handles the teen's need for independence will likely predict how the inevitable separation will play out as the young person moves ahead. The anxious parent will create anxiety in the teen, the assured parent will provide assurance, and the controlling parent will likely create rebellion. The parent will have her own set of feelings and issues that are reactive to her child's growing up and moving forward. If she is not aware of the impact that her feelings and behaviors have on her child, the scenario that gets played out may be fraught with turmoil as the parent places her worries on the youngster. Younger parents who are watching their first child move toward independence may not have the same level of self-awareness, understanding, and maturity as persons in midlife. Those who have lived decades may have come to see the process of the life cycle more fully and will be more ready to see their children move into their own adulthood. Younger parents may grieve more over the loss of their little child, and letting go could be more difficult. This picture is not universal, and many young parents will master the separation/individuation of their children with grace. However, midlife parents are more likely to be ready to watch their children propel themselves into the world.

If the parent is wise, he will see the prom as an opportunity to let the ties slacken so that his child can practice independence while still living at home. This parent will have been allowing other practice events to take place all through the high school years, with the prom as culmination. His child will have been coached in the pressures of drugs, alcohol, and sex, and he will know that it is time he trusts his child. Some teens will crash and burn and learn important life lessons. Others will sail gracefully through their first trial at young adulthood, with their parents watching from the stands and assisting or applauding as necessary. It is midlife parents who will have the longevity of years and likely the perspective to look back and see the need for letting go.

The art of letting go begins early, with the child's skinned knee. The parent's job is to hold and comfort the child and then to send her back out onto the playground. The child does not really belong to the parent, as hard a concept as that is to grasp. The child is her own person, cared for by the parent and moving into her own life of self-determination. The more mature the parent, the easier it will be to grasp this concept and be ready when the time comes to help the child launch into the world.

The move to college is one of the true marks of young adulthood, and the letting go can be challenging for parents.[6] Parents' feelings can be complex as the young adult moves out of home for the first time, whether the parents are young or older. Younger parents may grieve the loss of their child as he moves out of the house; in contrast, older parents may breathe a sigh of relief that their child has been successfully launched into the world. This is not to say that younger parents may not feel some relief and that older parents may not feel some loss. However, it is likely that the older the parent is, the more inevitable the launching will seem.

Research indicates significant correlation between parents' affective responses and children's coping.[7] Research also shows direct correlation between the family environment and children's social functioning.[8] The importance of the parents' response to their children cannot be overstated; stress levels in the home should be minimized whenever possible. This research speaks to the fact that parents need to have their own lives in order to be the best possible caregivers and role models for their children. By the time an individual has reached midlife and chosen to become a parent, that person will likely have gotten many individual issues identified and resolved. This having been accomplished, the individual will make a better parent, with the skills to manage stress and with resources for support in place.

FINANCIAL DILEMMAS

Money makes the world go around—or so many of our children may believe. When the Baby Boomers were children, they rode their bikes or played games outside, such as hide-and-seek, until dusk. They visited neighbors' homes on rainy days and played with an old train set or Barbie and Ken dolls for hours on end. For the really lucky kids, Mom or Dad would make popcorn or hot chocolate, and then they would entertain themselves. Expensive electronic gadgets that seem absolutely necessary to children in today's generation did not exist 30 years ago. The Baby Boomers did not go to the movies each week and routinely eat dinner out with their parents. They also did not "have to have" the latest fashion in designer tween and teen clothes because these fashion lines had not yet been developed. In the era of the advertisement, the Sandwich Generation is faced constantly with promotions for new products designed to appeal to their children. These children see the ads, talk to their friends whose parents may have purchased these products, and come to believe that they must also have the products to fit in.

The U.S. Department of Agriculture reports that the average American family will spend $269,520 to raise a child from birth through age 17. This study did not include the cost of private schools or a college education; rather, this estimate included only the basics of child rearing: housing, food, clothes, health care, and entertainment.[9] The cost of a college education can easily add $100,000, and after college, young adults may need help in purchasing a first home, as median single-family home prices now exceed $200,000 in many places.[10] This all adds up to a tidy sum of money.

For those in midlife who are also caring for and supporting their elders, saving for college for their children and preparing for their own retirement can seem to be an insurmountable task. Most parents want to provide their children with the best in life. When they are midlife parents, they must often make choices between what they have planned to do for themselves in their fifties and what they can now do for their children and parents. That longed-for yearly vacation to Europe or a sunny Caribbean island may need to be put on the back burner. The children may need braces or have a sports camp they want to attend. Sometimes the basic costs of clothing and food for a family can eat up any savings put aside for travel or leisure. The wise midlife parent will have done some financial planning earlier in her life and will have some savings put aside for her family needs. However, not all events can be planned for, and as the reality of time sets in during the middle years, an internal conflict can develop. The parent begins to understand that she will not have forever to get to Italy or to have that new car she has always planned for in her future. Suddenly, her child's college career is looming ahead, and she has the current day-to-day financial needs of her children. How can all the needs possibly be met?

Financial dilemmas and problems at midlife may be one of the factors that can propel a parent into the much-discussed midlife crisis. As the parent comes to understand that his needs may have to be put aside and once again postponed so he can to meet the needs of his children or aging parents, disappointment and even depression can set in. The midlife parent has worked for several decades with the hope that he will be able to settle into the middle years and put his life on cruise control. What he finds is something much different. The emotional needs of his children continue and require attention. The financial responsibility of being a parent drains the resources that he might have used for himself and his retirement. Midlifers begin to look at extending their employment when they had hoped to retire early. Reality is harsh.

This may seem to be a bleak picture. As with all things, there is an alternate way to look at how to manage finances so that they do not become the blow that buries the parents' dreams for themselves. It is especially important that parents keep their own dreams and plans; in doing so, they will then have the energy and willingness to provide for their children and elders.

The first step in addressing a frightening financial picture is to soothe oneself and use positive self-talk that it will work out—because it will. Yes, children need an endless supply of new boots as their feet grow and larger clothes as they grow taller. These are needs that must be filled. There must also be food on the table at night and a warm breakfast in the morning. Braces may be a necessity. School activities may cost money. Elderly parents may need home help to get through their day, which will also require financial assistance. The basic needs must be met. However, the parent's essential job must be to pare down to necessities and then learn to say no. Two functional pairs of jeans and three tops are adequate for a child or teen; a good pair of boots and a winter coat can be purchased that will last two seasons instead of one. Designer clothing is not necessary. The parent needs to create basic dinners at home instead of eating out—or eat out once a month instead of every week. As the parent learns to be frugal and to cut costs, the children learn a valuable lesson. The environment will reap the benefits as clothes are recycled and less is made into more. If one's children "must" have a certain item, then they can earn it by taking on tasks that help the family and by doing chores, such as emptying trash, dusting, and setting the dinner table, around the house. This teaches children the value of work and money and gives them pride in what they can provide for themselves. Some parents may not have any additional money, and this will need to be communicated to the children. If this is the case, parents can assist their children in locating neighborhood "jobs" such as snow shoveling, pet sitting, or babysitting to earn the extra cash they need.

Parents who have frank discussions with their children about finances and what they are saving for will be doing their children a service. It is important not to frighten the children into believing the family is in debt. However, children who gain an understanding of costs and savings will generally have a better sense of how to provide for themselves when they are launched into the world. Assisting children in opening bank accounts through which they can watch their allowance and gift money grow is a wonderful lesson in savings.

The parents must also be sure to put aside money for themselves. It may be a smaller amount than they had once hoped to save, but they must persevere in this matter. Otherwise, resentment will set in, and that despair about the self can take over. A good rule of thumb for parents is to have one night out a month without the children; dinner and a movie or any enjoyed activity is important for both single parents and couples to manage their perspectives and to keep hold of their own identities within the family. Additionally, at midlife, one parental vacation should be planned and looked forward to each year. This vacation does not have to be an around-the-world trip, but it should have some of the elements of a good getaway, even if it is only for a long weekend in the next state. Finally, parents need to put aside some money each month in an account solely for themselves and their own imaginings. While saving for the kids' college and helping the elderly through the aging process, midlifers also need to attend to their own needs. Individuals in the middle years need to be vigilant about their own paths, as well as the paths of their loved ones. They need to think positively, cut back financially in some areas regarding others (that new iPod their teen wants is not a necessity), and continue to build their own place and adventures on the planet. If they do not, life will begin to feel like a drain, and everyone, including themselves, will suffer.

HOPE FOR THE FUTURE

Yes, the children *will* launch! All the hard work and the love and the trials will pay off when productive young adults make their way into the world. These young people will no longer need their parents in the ways they once did, and late midlife parents will be able to finally focus on themselves. In some cases, the launched children will begin to give back in unexpected ways. As these new adults become kings and queens of their own financial kingdoms, they may surprise their beloved parents with a dinner out or even a trip to that lovely, dreamed about island. They may drop by and do the yard work and the heavy lifting that parents used to be able to manage on their own. The cycle begins again, with the children caring for the parents in small ways as they build their own lives. If Grandma and Grandpa are still living, oftentimes the launched children will take over some of the caregiving for their parents, transporting grandparents to the doctor, helping with meals and chores, and visiting.

Once the children have launched, late midlife individuals are left to fulfill their dreams. The days of wiping tears from eyes, attempting to help with homework, and preparing for proms and college are done. At first, the empty nest can feel as overwhelming as the noise and the demands that once were there. However, with time the parents will adjust to the quiet and the new rhythm of the reclaimed home.

The empty nest has its own set of psychological variables that midlife parents must face. Some parents relish the idea of having their lives and space back to themselves. Others parents fear the void and possible loneliness that may accompany their children's departure. Regardless, the time will come when the young adults launch, and the midlifers will once again be masters of their own universe.

Launching a young adult into the world is yet another developmental milestone for the parent. Marriage, home ownership, pregnancy, birth, possible divorce, and employment choices are all developmental milestones of the younger adult. As one faces midlife and beyond, new milestones exist.

These can include parenting at midlife, caring for elders, launching children, downsizing, and considering retirement.

As the children leave, not only is space left in the home, but also psychological space is left for the parents to design a revised life. Some natural grieving may come with this process as the parents adapt to the loss of the child around the house and at the dinner. The parents may even miss the general chaos the child created. Once the reality sets in that the child has grown up and left home, the parents have their own life and choices to consider. Some parents change their children's rooms into guest rooms or home offices as a real or symbolic gesture that their children have moved on, and so are they. Other parents create a shrine to their launched child by never changing the room and strategically placing old stuffed animals, dolls, and train tracks around the room for when their young adult returns for visits. Some parents decide to move entirely and downsize so their lifestyles will be more easily affordable.

Building the future and finding hope in the passage of children to the outside world are a wonderful way to celebrate the accomplishments of being a successful parent. The children have been launched! They are in the world and will make their own way. They will return to visit and perhaps build their own families. Grandchildren may be in the future. Celebrating the life cycle can be unique for each parent as each child leaves home.

The first step in the celebration of the future is to make it a conscious celebration. So many times in life these passages occur without acknowledgment or review. Sending a child to college or to a first apartment is an event for the parent as well as for the young adult. If the child comes from an intact family, the couple should find a way to mark the new era they are entering together. They can do this in simple ways, such as a quiet, uninterrupted candlelight dinner or a night on the town with friends. If the young adult is being launched from a single-parent home, the same suggestions apply: a quiet candlelight dinner or a night out. Other markers can be simple: a long bubble bath at the end of the move, a lengthy telephone call with a best friend, plans for the weekend. The important matter to keep in mind is to make the celebration conscious—to look back at the successes that have occurred over the years that have gotten the child to this place in time and to congratulate oneself on a job well done!

After the dust settles, the future will look different. Mornings and evenings will change without the house being full of young people. Breakfast will be for one or two rather than the family. There will now be more time for exercise, gardening, and reading. The television remote will be sitting on the couch waiting for the parents to choose what they want to watch. There will be many more small quiet moments. At first, this may feel uncomfortable. The house has rocked with life for the past 20 years, and suddenly the quiet may feel odd. As time proceeds and the young adult comes back on weekends or holidays to visit, a new rhythm will develop. Within that rhythm will likely be part of the new life plan that the parent is designing for herself. Again, making the plan conscious is a good choice; rather than stepping into a void without a road map, it can be most helpful to create a design.

The plan can include the daily routine, as well as special and future events or hopes. Looking forward to the future and imagining what it might look like in five years is a good place to start. The parent can start by taking out pen and paper and writing a wish list with two columns. The first column is for how each day might look, embellishing on the wishes that have been held at bay for many years. The second column is for the bigger picture, such as designing living space, moving, taking trips, building a small business, and embarking on creative ventures. See the examples below.

Daily Routine
- Sleep until seven
- Breakfast with my husband/read paper
- Work
- After work, meet my husband at the gym
- After exercise, have a glass of wine at the wine bar with my husband
- Cook dinner together/eat
- Have a bath, read, watch TV
- In bed with my husband or a book

Big Picture
- Travel locally once a month
- Downsize home to a condo
- Adopt a dog
- Take a vacation once every other year
- Build a ceramics business
- Join a book club

The plans for the daily routine can vary on the weekends and can be as long or short as the parent likes; the exercise is meant to build excitement and hope for the future and what can be accomplished. These accomplishments do not need to be huge events, such as starting a new business. Often, the most satisfaction in a new lifestyle can come from the cherished little things that there is now time to enjoy. Before, when the children were at home and their needs took precedence, it was difficult to find time to read a book (or even skim a magazine) or get to the gym regularly. It was likely impossible to have a quiet daily breakfast with one's partner or to read the paper. These are the joys that can be found in the quiet spaces that are left.

OUR CHILDREN, REVISITED

Children are the ones that can give us hope. As midlifers watch their parents fail and grow older, it is the children who are embracing life and tackling all the things that make each day vibrant. They are the opposite side of the coin of their aging grandparents. As the elders become frailer and need greater care, the youth grow into independence and begin to flourish. Watching them can instill hope during the midlife years as middle-aged individuals come to terms with the universal loss of their parents. The life cycle can seem cruel as it takes away the ones who have loved us and provided comfort when we were children. The grief we experience from this tremendous loss of our own parents at midlife often leaves us feeling like we are orphans in the world. Yet this grief can be mitigated by the love of our offspring. The cycle of life has its mystery and its beauty. If we allow it, we can find some comfort in the flow of the universe.

In the next chapter, the care and complications of helping elderly parents in their exit from the world are addressed. Underlying this inevitable exit there lies a deep sadness felt by both the elder as he emotionally prepares to die and the adult children who love him. It is the children who can remind the grieving adult that there is a continuity of life. They continue to need their parents, and the adults rise above their own grief to remember their children even in the throes of watching their own parents die. Children find laughter, continue routines, and provide love and consistency, all of which help the parents to remember that they need to remain open to life.

That children need their parents to be available to them even in times of greatest trauma and loss is a lesson that needs to be emphasized. The remarkable thing in this is that children, as they are cared for, will also provide the deepest solace in times of loss.

It is appropriate for parents to express sadness and hurt when loss or trauma occurs rather than to pretend that nothing significant has occurred.

This behavior will model for the children that feelings are acceptable, that they can also cry and be sad, and that the world will continue on. Children can be invited to be a part of the closing rituals in a grandparent's life. They can attend services (they should be offered the choice), write cards, visit the gravestone with gifts, and make memory books with their parents.

As the family navigates through the loss of an elder, its members can come to realize just how precious life is, and their valuing of each other may become more conscious and profound. Parents realize how important it is to say what needs to be said in the moment, and children, on some level, begin to realize that their own parents will not be with them forever. They may need reassurance and comfort, and they will also provide comfort to their parents, as they move more quickly and easily back into the world following loss.

Every day it is important to celebrate our children—to take moments out of the busy daily routine and focus on the goodness and joy that young people bring to the world. As important as it is to take these moments to recognize what is good, it is equally important to verbalize to children of all ages how much they are loved and valued. As parents rush through the day working, caring for elders, and trying to breathe for themselves, it can be difficult to remember that children need nurturance and verbal reassurance. They do not need to perfect, just as parents will not be perfect. They need to be good enough, and if their parents are good enough, the children will flourish and grow in a manner that is positive and rewarding for themselves and others.

There are little things to do that can make all the difference in providing attention and love for children. They can include the following:

- Sit with your child at breakfast every morning. Make it a ritual with a special breakfast meal on certain days (for example, make her chocolate chip pancakes on Wednesday).
- Say a word of praise about something (small or significant) each morning at breakfast. Make your child feel seen and loved with words that show you notice him.
- Put a note in your child's backpack or lunch once in a while.
- Have dinner consistently at the same time every night when possible. Use the mealtime to discuss your child's day and help her review things she feels proud about.
- Play a game with him after dinner.
- Help with homework; do not nag about it.

- Assign chores and give praise every day when the chores are done.
- Make sure your child writes thank you notes; help her.
- Watch TV shows that are appropriate for your child.
- Have a consistent bedtime hour and sit with your child when he goes to bed; ask him how his day was and what he did well and what he might like to do better tomorrow. Talk about what you and your child are grateful for that day. Say prayers if suited for your family.

These are just a few of the small things that parents can do to ensure good enough parenting that will "fill up" both the child and the parent and build intimacy and love. There are many other consistent, positive rituals that parents can develop that do not need to be extravagant or time consuming but that are important to the growth of the child.

Give love, and it will be received, internalized, and given back. A wonderful cycle of replenishment can be created that can be reenacted for generations to come.

FOUR

Our Parents

CASE EXAMPLE: REVERSING ROLES

Vanessa watches her father working in the garden and feels angry as she sees him putter with her flowers. Her anger overtakes her at times, and once she becomes aware she is angry, the feeling turns to guilt. Vanessa berates herself for harboring old resentments regarding a fragile old man.

Samuel looks up at the sun and feels the summer heat on his face. He loves the garden because it feels to him like he is close to the earth, where his wife was buried months ago. After the funeral, he moved in with his daughter, Vanessa, and her husband, and since the move, he has spent as much time outside as he can. He does not think that his broken heart will ever heal, and he knows he is simply waiting to join his wife in whatever afterlife exists. Samuel married his wife, Patrice, when he returned from his time in the Army after World War II. She was his only sweetheart, and they had one daughter, Vanessa, and one son, named after him. His son, Samuel II, lives on the East Coast, and they speak by telephone once a week and on special occasions. Vanessa is the only family he has left besides his boy.

Samuel knows he is a tough old bird, and he feels like an imposition on his daughter. He had refused to leave the home that he and Patrice had lived in for 55 years until he had suffered a stroke. Having to leave his own home feels like another blow. He hates being dependant on his daughter and son-in-law. He can no longer drive, and he feels like his only escape from his daughter's home is in the yard. Samuel is now eating the food that his daughter prepares for her family rather than the meals he is accustomed to eating. He uses her kitchen to get his coffee and uses the brands of bread and milk that are in her refrigerator. Vanessa does the shopping and purchases the toothpaste that her family uses, not what Samuel prefers. He has his own room with a sitting area so he can watch the television programs he likes, and he is grateful for this last bit of independence.

Samuel sighs and remembers his wife. He wonders if he had been the best husband that he could have been and often finds himself having regrets about how he treated her. Patrice had been a good soul, and he knows that he had been demanding and cross at times. That did not mean he had not loved her; it was just his way. But he wonders now if he should have told her he loved her more, maybe thought to buy her little things and help at home. He misses the way she smelled of lilacs. Sometimes he can imagine the fragrance when he is in bed at night. Patrice was the better part of him, and Samuel knows this, but he regrets that he never told her. Patrice would intervene when he would drink too much and hit the children, and Samuel tries to shake off the memory of the time Patrice had gotten in his way and he had knocked her down. He recalls that Vanessa had been screaming and Samuel II had been cowering at the top of the stairs, fearful that he would be beaten. Samuel tries to close his mind to the past and justify his behaviors to himself. If the kids had only obeyed more quickly, if they had done as they were told, none of the arguments would have occurred. There are times now that he can see anger in Vanessa's eyes when she looks at him. He sees anger and then pity. He is ashamed of his broken body and ashamed of the anger in her eyes. Samuel feels useless, and sometimes the old demons of rage surface within him, and he lashes out with words at his daughter. He cannot apologize. The words stick inside his mouth.

Vanessa watches her father some more from behind the curtain in the window. She wonders why it could not have been her father who had died first, so her mother could have enjoyed some of her life, even if it was at the end. Vanessa had watched her mother take care of her father all the years of her life. Samuel had been demanding of Patrice, and when he would drink, he would become abusive. When Vanessa and her brother were children, they had feared the broken old man who was now in her garden. He could change in a minute's time from a reticent person into a raging bull that put terror in their hearts. Even at his best, when he was sober, Samuel had not been an attentive father or husband. He had been self-absorbed and self-important. Samuel had acted as if his job had been the one thing he loved, and he would pump himself up when he talked about it. As Vanessa grew older, she had had less patience in listening to him. She thought his job as a bank manager was ridiculously stupid, and she could not understand his pride. She thought that it was no big deal that her father had to open the bank doors in the morning and lock them at night. A monkey could be trained to do that!

Vanessa recalls one incident that seems to pop into her mind at the most inopportune moments. She remembers the day clearly; she can almost feel the coolness in the fall air. She was in her teens, and she had just finished setting the dinner table. Samuel had been sitting in the living room, drinking his second scotch, and Patrice had been finishing up the side dishes. Vanessa's brother had come through the front door and dropped his backpack on the living room floor. On this particular night, that was all it had taken for Samuel to spiral into a rage. Samuel II had lifted his hands to defend himself, and Samuel had thought that his son was trying to strike him, so he had grabbed the fireplace poker and swung it at his son's legs. Samuel II had toppled to the ground before Patrice could get to the room to intervene. Samuel II had been bleeding badly, and his father had appeared as if he was going to strike his son again. Vanessa recalled screaming and hearing her mother yell to call the police. Vanessa could barely remember making the telephone call to 911. She had tried to help her mother get the poker from her father, and her next memory was of the police coming in with their guns drawn.

The aftermath of that incident was a blur. Samuel II had been taken to the hospital, with Vanessa and her mother following, and her father had been scolded by the police but not arrested. It had not felt like reality to Vanessa. She remembers that she had been most worried about the family cat, which had been left at home with her father. She had worried that he would kill it. Samuel II's leg had almost been severed, and he had needed surgery. Vanessa recalls having been terrified and not wanting to return home.

The family had never spoken a word about what had happened. Other than the fact that a state worker had been sent to the house to interview them, they had gone about their lives without any noticeable changes. Vanessa never saw the state report, but it did not change things either. Samuel II had walked on crutches for several weeks and to this day has a slight limp from his father's attack. Vanessa is sure that her brother has never forgiven Samuel, and she is not sure that she has either.

Having her father living in her home is complicated for Vanessa because of her anger at him for his past behaviors. She tries to lock the bad memories away, but they surface at times without her permission. Vanessa can become overwhelmed with anger at her father, and then she slides into feeling pity for the old man who is now so helpless. She is thankful that her husband acts as a buffer between them when the tension becomes observable. Her father feels awkward accepting her help because he is so proud. She feels ambivalent about giving her help, caught between feeling responsible and angry. Vanessa is aware that, if the places were reversed and it was her mother who was still living, she would feel differently. Vanessa would have loved the opportunity to take care of her mother, spoil her, and spend time with her.

Vanessa now has the responsibility for caring for her father in a way that he never cared for her. She makes his meals, does his laundry, takes him to a multitude of doctors' appointments, arranges for home help when she has to be at work, and plays cribbage with him at night. When she was a child, he had never spent any of his time really caring for her, and she is aware of this. As she moves through her day, Samuel feels like one more chore she has to manage. In fact, he takes away some of the precious time that she used to spend with her husband or just reading and relaxing. It is conflicting for Vanessa to be taking on the role of her father's caregiver.

Vanessa sits down in her kitchen and thinks about her life. She is 52, and she has a fairly good marriage and two children of her own, who are away at college. Her work is satisfying, and she has several good friends. Her struggles now seem to focus on this new role of taking care of her father and the memories he brings up for her. As she looks back at her childhood, she can see how his drinking and other behaviors have influenced her ways of functioning as an adult. She is aware she has sharp bursts of anger at her husband and children, sometimes for small incidents. She also knows that, at times, she isolates herself more than she should, and her husband calls her controlling when they argue. Lately, by watching her father on a daily basis, Vanessa has become more aware that her past has influenced how she is today in the world.

Vanessa wants to make some meaning of her memories and to make changes in her current behaviors, as she realizes that she does not want to be like her father. She is not sure how or where to start, but it is becoming clearer that her sharp, critical nature is unpleasant and hurtful. She finds herself feeling guilty when she snaps at her husband and when she is short with Samuel. Vanessa is aware that her father's life span is now limited, and she does not want to spend her last years with him feeling resentment for the past.

Vanessa thinks about attending counseling and begins to think about returning to church. While her husband and friends are good listeners, Vanessa feels like she needs something more, something bigger than herself to find her way. She stops into several local churches to see if any of them might be a good match for her beliefs. She finally decides to return to one of the churches she tried and continues attending each week. She builds a community of spiritual companions at the church and is able to begin to use her spirituality to find grace and forgiveness. It is not always perfect—*she* is not always perfect—but Vanessa knows she wants to make changes, and she keeps at it.

Many positives come from Vanessa's experience at midlife with her father. As being with him brings back memories of her past, Vanessa comes to understand that many of her current behaviors result from her childhood. While she is not pleased with these behaviors, she sets forth to change them. As she works on taming her sharp and critical self, her relationship with her husband improves and deepens. Vanessa is also able to make amends to her children for the times she has been too harsh with them, and her relationships with them soften and become more loving. Vanessa looks deeper into her family history and learns that her father had been raised in an abusive household, and this understanding also helps to soften Vanessa's feelings for Samuel. As Vanessa looks to her future, she feels lighter, more positive, and better about herself. Her relationship with Samuel creates less inner turmoil for her, and she finds herself interested in learning more about him and his life story. Through the church, Vanessa also connects Samuel to three World War II veterans who come by to visit and play weekly cribbage with her father while they talk. Vanessa is rewarded by seeing her father connect with others who had experienced war, by learning more about her father, and by regaining some of the private time for herself and her husband that she had lost.

THE BOND: POSITIVE, NEGATIVE, AND CORRECTIVE

One of the great complications of midlife can be the relationship that the individual has or has had with her parents. This parent-child relationship is forged during the early years and is one of the most important relationships that a person can have, as it facilitates the development of the individual personality.

When the bond with one's parents is a strong and positive attachment, then all good things are possible. Parents who are able to provide their children with love, affection, corrective experiences, and a solid sense of self as they are developing will likely reap the rewards of a loving relationship with their children.

Brent Mallinckrodt notes that early relationships have far-reaching consequences for healthy adult functioning. Early parental bonds mold the view of the developing child in the social world. The development of a child into a person who views himself as an effective participant in a social world that is generally responsive to his efforts depends in part on how responsive his early caregivers have been to him.[1] Conversely, a child who has had unresponsive parents may not feel as if he is an effective participant in life. This feeling will affect his self-esteem and overall functioning in the world.

The adult child who has felt loved and nurtured by her parents throughout her life will likely emerge into midlife experiencing a positive bond in her relationships with her mother and father. Positive bonds relate consistently to self-efficacy, care, and social self-efficacy (p. 458).[2] Abraham Maslow noted that, when the child's basic needs are met, she has the ability to actualize her own potential. Maslow went on to note that the self-actualized person is one who is creative, optimistic, spontaneous, and likely to have peak experiences. Additionally, the self-actualized person is described as having more ability to transcend difficult life circumstances such as anxiety, depression, and physical disabilities. This individual is able to maintain a rich, meaningful life and live to the fullest potential while she continues to grow and develop.[3]

Many of the causes of maladaptive functioning in adulthood stem both directly and indirectly from early relationships with one's caregivers. If one has maladaptive functioning, it is likely that many of one's relationships will be impaired. Included in these impaired relationships could be dysfunction in the relationship with one's parents. In other words, the way one was raised will impact both the desire and the ability one has to care for one's own parents.

An individual's positive early bond with his parents will likely come full circle in his relationship with his parents as an adult, a relationship built on a foundation of love, affection, and positive regard. The adult child who has been loved in a good enough manner by his parents will find himself taking on the caregiver role for them in later life, an act that gives back some of the love and affection that he received as a child.[4] This loved adult will likely be well adjusted, have solid emotional resources, and feel a desire to do what is best for his aging parents. The adult who has been raised in a loving environment may feel many of the pressures of any midlife individual who has the responsibility of caring for both his own children and his aging parents. However, this person will be less likely to feel bitterness and anger over his burden.

A negative early bond with one's parents will also likely impact how the adult child responds to her parents' aging. The individual raised by parents who were unavailable, neglectful, or abusive will certainly experience ambivalence in the caretaking of her elders. At midlife, this adult may be less emotionally stable, have more disrupted relationships, and feel less desire to care for elder parents who were not kind to her as a child. It is a predicament for anyone to be placed in the position of having to take care of those who have been cruel or abandoning. Anger and resentment may cloud the adult child's ability to find compassion and may make taking care of her aging parents an impossible task. Behaviors that were learned from her parents, paradoxically, may emerge to play out in a reverse manner. The same early environment of negligence may be reenacted between child and parent; however, this time the parent is the one to suffer the indifference. The adage "what goes around comes around" may turn out to be all too true.

Either children are raised with good enough parenting, or they are raised in a home in which they are faced with neglect or abuse. There is certainly a continuum from a warm and healthy home environment to an abusive home, and many other factors may mitigate negative early parenting. For example, a loving grandparent, teacher, or neighbor can positively impact a child. This influence may be so profound that even abuse at home is softened, and the child grows hope and resilience through the affection of someone outside the home. This child, who soon grows into an adult, can develop the ability to forgive his parents' behaviors and correct flaws in his own personality.

The creation of a forgiving attitude toward one's parents must be a conscious endeavor. The adult child must be able to look at her life experience and acknowledge that she was parented in less-than-perfect ways. She must then make a conscious decision to attempt to do things differently, regardless of the past. This process of change can include self-awareness, personal therapy, and active reflection. The decision to attempt to find love and caring for estranged parents who have been unavailable or abusive can be a challenging concept. The good news is that the adult child who chooses this path will reap the benefits of greater self-actualization and self-respect.

Forgiveness is a spiritual matter. It takes fortitude and an amazing ability to look past hurts and then to forgive. Forgiveness is not rational, nor is it a required act. Instead, forgiveness is an act that comes from the soul in the face of all adversities; it rises up from the ashes of abuse, terror, neglect, and horror to become an unimaginable feat of supreme grace. It is a conscious event, designed by those who have been offended, to move forward and show acceptance and even love in the face of cruelty. In fact, forgiveness is possibly the most remarkable quality to which the human species can aspire.[5]

To forgive one's parents is not a universal phenomenon; it is chosen as an opportunity by some and forsaken as an impossibility by others. In those who choose not to forgive, the ability to care for their parents will be at best ambivalent. These adult children who choose not to forgive may have their own very good reasons; their abuse may have been too

egregious or their pain too great to allow them to move past it. The choice
to forgive is unique to each person and set of circumstances. The act of
forgiveness requires that the individual reappraise the hurt and go through
a shift in how he thinks and feels about the offender.[6] This shift can
require a great deal of emotional energy and dedication.

PHYSICAL AND EMOTIONAL CARE OF ELDERLY PARENTS

Roles are clearly reversed when our parents age. With advanced years,
our parents become increasingly more physically fragile. They may fall
and break a hip, develop Alzheimer's disease, or suffer chronic pain from
any variety of illnesses. Emotionally, many elderly individuals become vulnerable to anxiety and depression. Their friends have died, they are losing
their teeth and bladder control, and they ultimately have trouble managing
all the tasks that they have been masterful at all their lives. Between the
physical changes in their bodies and the multiple losses they experience
socially, it is no wonder they can become depressed. Many elderly lose
their life partners to death or the nursing home. More than six million older
Americans receive some form of daily in-home care, and half of those over
85 years of age need some sort of assistance with activities of daily living
such as eating, toileting, or dressing.[7] Aging is a concept that we do not like
to think about until it is upon us; however, the reality is that all of us will
age and face the same circumstances at life's end.

Reverting to many of the early phenomena with which each person
began life in childhood becomes a reality as every individual nears the
end of her life. Help is needed with dressing, eating, getting to appointments with the doctor or the dentist, and even managing or getting to
social events. The elderly, like children, are more vulnerable and less able
to manage life without help. Children begin life dependent on their parents
for food, shelter, and the basics needed for survival. In old age, the same
needs arise, and the adult children of these elderly must take on the role
that was once held by the parents who are now failing.

This role reversal from being the one who is cared for to being the caregiver is never welcomed. It can be greeted with disbelief by the adult child
who cannot grasp that his cherished parent can no longer care for *him*. A
torrent of feelings may accompany the reality that now he must care for
the parent. Feelings of sadness, anxiety, frustration, exhaustion, and, at
times, resentment are not uncommon for the adult caregiver. Even adult
children who realize that someday their parents will age and need their
care are surprised when it actually happens. How can our parents abandon
us? Why can't Mom still listen to my problems, console me, and help me

solve them like she always has? Why can't Dad drive to the pharmacy and pick up that prescription? How can I possibly fit one extra thing into my busy schedule?

Those elderly who have provided good enough parenting to their children will be more likely to reap the rewards of loving caregivers in the form of their grown children. The roles can reverse slowly as the adult child begins to care for her parent. This does not happen all at once, and sometimes the change is initially so slow and insidious that it is barely noticed. This parent-child role reversal may begin with small things as the adult child periodically takes the aging parent to a doctor's appointment, picks up groceries on occasion, or helps with bills that now seem confusing. When complications increase, as they naturally will through the aging process, the adult child may take on more caregiving tasks or help her parents move to a nursing home or an assisted-living facility. Caring for one's parents or assisting them with the move to a facility can be exhausting and emotionally draining. However, if the relationship between parent and child is a positive one, the hurdles will be managed with compassion and greater rewards for all. In the beginning stages of later life and aging, there may be time for the parent and adult child to make preparations for what is to come. Guardianship can be arranged and finances protected before significant decline occurs. Conversations can occur that take into account the parent's wishes for the time when care is needed. If the relationship between parent and child has been open, it is likely these conversations will not be tremendously difficult.

The ability of the adult child to provide either physical or emotional care in the home is dependant on many circumstances. The adult must first be willing and able to provide the care, and the illness or disability of his parent must be manageable at home. In the best of circumstances, the discussion about the move to a facility can be traumatic. The aging parent will want to remain in the home for as long as possible, and this will often be dependent on the resources available for support.

Elderly individuals who do not have caregivers that are willing or able to provide assistance will be dependent upon the state for help. Without the family and social resources that provide home help, these people will likely be less able to remain at home as long as those who have supports. This is not necessarily a negative situation; however, the elders in this circumstance will have fewer choices.

For most elders, there will come a time when their children can no longer care for them in the home even with the best of parent-child relationships. This can be a traumatic realization for both the elder and the adult child. The conversation regarding a move from one's home can be painful for the aging person who has already lost so much. For the adult child, there is often great remorse and guilt that she cannot do more to keep her loved parent in his own home, or even living with her. Preparation for this event is crucial. Early efforts to research appropriate facilities will provide the caregiver with important information about opportunities for the best care. Additionally, and perhaps more importantly, the action of looking at facilities well in advance of the parent's need to be moved can be helpful in preparing the adult child emotionally.

IMPENDING LOSS

The impending loss of the parent certainly becomes clearer as aging takes it path. Facing the death of one's parents can be an awakening to the knowledge that sometime in the approaching future one's champions and greatest fans will be gone. Many adult children feel like orphans for the first time in their lives as they come to understand that their parents are no longer there to support or take care of them. The universe shifts as this realization dawns, and the adult child must find some way to come to terms with this loss.

Compounding the realization that one's parents are going to die is the often-simultaneous awareness that one's own life must, therefore, be finite. Many times individuals do not completely become aware of their own transitory place on the planet until they experience some great loss or other tragedy. With the knowledge that life is indeed finite, making each moment as rich and loving as possible becomes the goal. Understanding that loss is inevitable brings with it a great gift; making each interaction count as if it were the last can color each relationship with patience, meaning, and love.

As the days at the end of the life cycle dwindle, the luckiest individuals have the opportunity to forgive, create joint meaning, and say all the things that need to be said before the final hour.

Simple Tips to Cope with Life Loss

- *Stay in the moment whenever possible.* Do not focus on the past or what is to come. Be present with your loved one.
- *Manage your own fears about death and dying.* This might mean joining a group or seeking personal counseling. Losing a parent is a tremendous life event, and the grief can be complicated by ambivalence, anger, sadness, and fear.
- *Manage your own feelings about the past.* Unresolved feelings of anger at your parent may interfere with the ability to be loving and present as

she ages and needs help. Trying to work through these feelings with the parent may not be the best way (or time) to resolve them. A support group for caregivers or personal therapy may be helpful for the adult caregiver who is navigating these waters.

- *Recognize that your parent will not be here with you forever, and if you can, express your love often.* Many families do not openly express love. It may be challenging to change this pattern as your parent ages and faces death. Recognize that there will not be opportunities after he has died to tell him he is loved. Have courage and speak up.

- *Remember to say what needs to be said now.* There may not be another opportunity. It is a terrible thing to have a loved one pass and have things lingering that you wish you had said.

- *Be with your parent where she is.* Try to have patience and focus on what the parent can do, not what she cannot do. For example, the elderly parent with a poor memory may need to be reminded several times to eat food that has been served. Work on patience, stay in the moment with your parent, and lovingly continue the reminders to eat. It is in just that moment, and in that kindness, that meaning can be established between the aging parent and adult child.

- *Touch your parent more than you usually might.* Touch can be very important to the elderly. For the aging adult who has lost memory, the presence of touch will still remind him he is loved. Hold his hand, look in his eyes, rub his arm, and hug him as much as possible. Whether or not your parent's memory is still intact, the sensation of touch will be meaningful—and the words of love and affection invaluable.

- *Take care of yourself.* It is crucial that caregivers make time for themselves to grieve the loss of the parent they knew, to rejuvenate, and to find time to play and laugh. Watching a parent's slow decline makes it clear just how short life is, and this lesson is important to heed in one's own life.

- *Celebrate small things, both past and present.* Each small accomplishment can bring a smile to an elder's face if it is acknowledged. If your parent is able to dress herself or remembers to brush her teeth, a recognition and small celebration are in order. Remember when you were a small child and your little successes were celebrated; it is now your turn to celebrate your parent's accomplishments.

- *Reminisce.* Most of the elderly love to recall their past, look at pictures, and be reminded of their youth. Make time to sit with your parent and listen or look at photographs.

- *Do not be afraid to be silly.* Laugh a lot, do a silly dance, or wear funny glasses and see the response you will get from your elderly loved one.

- *Sing.* Many elderly people love to sing. Your parent may not remember the words to the song, but if you choose a song from his early years, he will hum along and be right in the moment with you.

- *Find joy.* It may be challenging to find those moments of joy when your loved one is requiring attention or is ill or when you are overwhelmed with the need to get to all the other tasks that await you. Try to stay in the moment and be grateful for that one minute that you have in the present with your loved one.

- *Get help when you need it.* Ask for help from a sibling, friend, or neighbor so you can take time for yourself. Hire respite care. Think about placement in an assisted-living facility or nursing home if the demands become overwhelming. Remembering to share the burden so that you do not become resentful is critical. Caregiving belongs to all members of the family system, not just one sibling. Ask for help from brothers or sisters even if they live at a distance. They can still contribute by making telephone calls to seek resources, providing financial support for help in the home, or offering emotional support to the primary caregiver and to the elder via telephone.

MANAGING THE BALANCE BETWEEN AGING PARENTS AND CHILDREN

The balancing act between caring for our parents and caring for our children is the theme of this book. In this chapter, the discussion relates directly to aging parents and how to find time for them while also parenting children still in the home. It is a precarious act; while there may be enough love to go around, having the energy to spread it can be compromised because there is simply so much to do.

Caring for elderly parents can be as demanding and as consuming as caring for children. Our elderly parents can regress and become more childlike as our youngsters age and become more mature, and issues surrounding both of these phenomena are multifaceted. As discussed, the aging individual may need more assistance with the basics of daily living, such as bathing, personal hygiene, and other tasks that were once simple. At the same time, the children in the home may be moving out of the phase when they need help in these basic areas, but other needs develop. The adult child may begin to care for her elder in some of the same ways she was, in the recent past, caring for her own children. The children are likely moving into a stage of greater independence, which brings its own challenges to parenthood. These tweens or teenagers need a different kind of parenting, which can involve hours of driving back and forth to school sports and other events, a watchful eye as they grow, and help preparing for college.

How can the adult caregiver manage it all? Is it humanly possible to be there for one's parents as they age and still perform all the same tasks that one has been responsible for all along? Life's tasks may have seemed overwhelming even before one's parents became infirm and vulnerable. Now the reality has set in, and the adult caregiver must mobilize. Action plans need to be set in place so that chaos does not set in; when chaos happens, none of the family members get their needs met, and the caregiver feels like he is failing both his parents and his children.

It becomes the task of the caregiver to be creative. In learning to think outside the box, the adult child will find ways to minimize her own work while facilitating connections with others. For example, encouraging one's children to spend time with their grandparents as part of a family cycle can be a wonderful way to teach children about empathy and giving. Children often love being in the role of the special one for their grandparents. When this connection is encouraged, the child will spend time with Grandma or Grandpa, and the parent may supervise but also get a much-needed hands-on break. The bond between grandparent and child will flourish, and both will be recipients of deeper love and meaning. Activities as simple as watching a movie together or sitting outside together while the child does homework can facilitate a bond. Elderly individuals want to be helpful and included. They will feel good about being engaged in their grandchildren's life and retain feelings of usefulness that can get lost as the years progress.

When the elderly parents live in the home with the extended family, it can be easier to include them in all aspects of the family's life. Dinner will likely be an event for the entire group, and the grandparent can be provided with a chore just like everyone else. It may be something as simple as asking him to wipe off the table after the meal, but it will help him to feel included and useful. The sit-down meal at the end of the day is still one of the most important rituals a family can embrace. It may be difficult to have everyone in the same place at the same time, especially with teenagers in the home; however, it is the one time that connection can be made and relationships solidified.

The caregiver needs to seek other creative ways to combine her children and her parents so that her time can be spent doing the other things that are required. For example, the grandparent may be the one who can be at home during after-school hours to supervise the children. "Supervision" may mean simply being present so that the younger ones are not alone in the house. The company of the children can stem the loneliness that the elderly may feel from being alone all day long while the adult is at work. Some grandparents may still be able to help with homework or play a game with their grandchildren during this time. When the grandparents are able or the children are old enough, simple chores can be left that will help the adult when she gets home. These chores can include doing the laundry, starting dinner, or vacuuming the rugs.

There may be times when the grandparent needs time and assistance from the adult child that will take away from the grandchildren's needs for attention. If this occurs in a two-parent home, some help can be gained from the spouse in meeting the needs of the children. Regardless, conversations should occur that teach the children that there will be times when Grandma or Grandpa will need Mom's or Dad's extra help. In this way, the children will be prepared and come to understand and develop patience. The adult child must remember to praise the children for giving him the time needed to attend to their grandparents—and to include them if they wish.

Special time can be created for both the elder and the children in the home so that everyone feels that they have the attention each human being craves and needs. It can be helpful for the parent to set a predetermined and consistent time each day with the children in the home. In that way, each child will know ahead of time that she will have her special moment with her parent at a predetermined hour. If the child is aware that her personal time is coming, it is likely that she will feel less resentment toward her grandparent for time taken away from her. Conversely, if the grandparent knows that he will have special time with his adult child, he will likely be less needy, have fewer health complaints, and be better adjusted.

As an example, a scheduled evening can begin with the dinner hour, during which everyone is present. After dinner cleanup, when all can be involved at some level, an hour can be set aside for a family game with the kids or help with homework. Following this hour, the grandparents can be helped by their adult child with getting ready for bed and enjoying an hour in front of the television or playing cards or looking at old pictures and talking. The third hour can be reserved for the children; it can be spent watching a TV show, talking, helping with a school project, or doing a craft. It may seem artificial to schedule the evening in such a manner, but in a busy blended family, the schedule helps everyone to know what to expect and when to expect it. This knowledge assists everyone in understanding that there will be time for each family member, however brief it may seem. Once the routine is established, there is a certain calm-ness that settles into the home, even for the busy caregiver. And no, the caregiver has not been forgotten. The next chapter will address self-care and survival for the people who do it all.

Many elderly do not reside in the home with the family. Other routines can be set up that match the particular situation. Schedules can provide everyone with the comfort and knowledge of what to expect and when to expect it. For example, family visitations may be scheduled with the grandparents twice a week, the adult child may stop in each day on the way home from work to check in with her loved ones, or any facsimile of such a routine can be devised that will be of tremendous help to all. It is not so critical what the routine is; simply the fact that there is a known routine provides consistency and comfort.

The world is an extremely busy place, and for the adults finding them-selves in the Sandwich Generation, the process of keeping a routine and schedule can be synonymous with maintaining sanity. In a busy day with multiple tasks to be accomplished, it can be comforting to have it all mapped out so that the adult caregiver can see what is coming next on the schedule. Without a schedule, pieces can get lost or forgotten, and family members can feel abandoned. It is also important to remember that there is help to be gained from asking others, and putting free time in the schedule for the self is as important as any other event.

Balancing the care of one's parents and one's children can feel over-whelming and exhausting. It is imperative that adult children who are caregivers find ways to care for themselves. The next chapter will address strategies with which those who are feeling overwhelmed by their multi-ple roles can soothe and care for themselves.

FIVE

The Self and the Importance of a Plan

CASE EXAMPLE: SINK OR SWIM?

The alarm clock seems to be a million miles away. Elizabeth feels around on her nightstand for the clock in the hope of shutting it off before she wakes her daughters, asleep in the next room. It is like trying to raise her arm from the depths of a heavy ocean, and she feels some longing to return to the dream state that has just been broken. She is aware she needs to get moving and propels herself into action. She thinks for a minute about how nice it would be to have a leisurely cup of coffee with her husband.

Two daughters, three cats, two elderly parents, and a busy job all beckon her to rise and greet the day. Her husband, still asleep in bed, would encourage her to roll over for a few minutes if he were awake. He shares all the household responsibilities with her now that he is partially retired, heaven bless him. Elizabeth does not know what she would do without his help. He does the laundry, sets the table, runs errands, and often prepares dinner for the family.

Elizabeth moves from the bed to the shower, with the smallest cat trailing her. This little kitty, Puffy Girl, is the one that is always getting in trouble, and she likes to share Elizabeth's morning shower. Puffy Girl will squeeze herself in between the shower curtain and liner and feel the warm water through the liner but never get wet. Elizabeth has to be sure to arrange the shower liner so that it protects Puffy from the water. With some humor, Elizabeth thinks to herself that even her shower is not sacred. The morning shower with her cat reflects how the rest of the day will go; everyone will want a piece of her until she finally tumbles back into bed at night.

Elizabeth's least favorite morning ritual is applying her makeup. As she has gotten older, she does not see as well, and she is always afraid she will leave big pink blush circles on her cheeks like the elderly people she sees at the supermarket. Her husband has risen by now, and the bathroom mirror is also fogged up by his shower, making the challenge of makeup application all the more frustrating. The other two cats, both boys, like to jump up on the sink during her makeup ritual, and while this is endearing, Elizabeth always has to put them down. She feels the first of many daily pangs of guilt at her bathroom sink each morning with her cats. She wishes she could give all those she loves more attention. She knows she has precious little time to devote to the animals and is glad that they are good company for each other.

Elizabeth kisses her husband through an opening in the shower curtain, and they exchange a few words about the daily chore list and expressions of love before she goes downstairs. As Elizabeth walks, her eyes adjust to the dark, and they sweep back and forth like a guard's spotlight, checking for anything out of place. Often, she will pick up discarded pieces of clothing or pages of homework that she will place by each person's breakfast setting to be taken care of before her family leaves the house. During her sweep, Elizabeth will see if there is a load of laundry that needs to be thrown in the washer or if the dishwasher or small trash receptacles need to be emptied. She also notes what might need to be accomplished in the evening, such as vacuuming, dusting, or any other chore. Elizabeth then quickly checks her email and makes a mental note of any correspondence that needs immediate attention when she gets to work. Sometimes while waiting for the coffee to brew, she responds to some of her email.

Her husband set the breakfast table the night before, and Elizabeth writes the family a love note saying good-bye and leaves it propped each morning on the table with the lunches she made the night before. She misses the breakfast hour with her family and wishes she could be with them. Elizabeth feeds the cats, empties the litter box, grabs her "to go" coffee cup and prepared lunch bag, and is out the door by 6:30.

Elizabeth is 53 years old. If anyone asked her, which they have not, she would say she is happy with her life. She has amazing 12-year-old twins, a wonderful marriage, and a fulfilling career. She is lucky to still have living parents with whom she can spend time.

Yet she is tired. The days are long and filled with taking care of everyone else. After her busy day at work, Elizabeth returns home to begin the routine of dinner, cleanup, homework, leftover chores and ironing, visits with her parents, and, finally, the glorious tumble into bed. And oh, isn't that tumble—her head hitting the soft pillow, the lights out, the cozying into the blankets—just the best thing in the world? Sometimes her husband will have turned on her electric blanket before she gets into bed, and it is always one of the best moments of her day to feel so loved.

How does Elizabeth find time for herself? How is it possible for Elizabeth to be happy when the world places so many demands on her? Elizabeth wonders how other mothers are able to manage all they juggle. She knows she is one of the luckier ones, as she has a partner to share her duties. Even with the help of her husband, Elizabeth often feels overwhelmed by the sheer volume of tasks that need to be completed in the day. It is difficult to make time for herself, her friends, and her hobbies. Elizabeth finds it challenging to even find time for a 30-minute walk each day. When she takes this time for herself, she feels like she is stealing precious moments from her children and parents.

The twins are at an active age and always want to be engaged in activities with their parents when possible. Elizabeth can become frustrated with their inability to entertain themselves, especially after she has spent time with them and they continue to want more. They seem like little empty vessels that she continues to need to fill with all her time and energy. Elizabeth struggles with guilt when she sets limits with them, but she has other responsibilities that need her attention.

Elizabeth's parents live across town. She has always been especially close to her mother. Lately, she feels as if her heart is slowly breaking as she watches her mother descend into Alzheimer's disease. This insidious disease was diagnosed a few years ago, and her mother is now unable to remember many daily functions or complete basic activities without cueing. Elizabeth's father is mentally robust; however, his body is frail, and Elizabeth is always fearful he will fall. She thinks that together her parents now make one strong parent, her father with his competent mind and her mother with her good physical health. Individually, they are each challenged by age in different ways.

The harder burden falls to her father, with the constant care he provides for Elizabeth's mother. In the back of Elizabeth's mind is always a worry that her father will become exhausted and overwhelmed. She tries to prepare meals for them on Sunday that will last the week so her father does not have to cook. Weeknights Elizabeth settles her own children down for the evening after dinner and drives to her parents' house to spend an hour with them. Her husband sometimes visits her parents during the day and takes care of odd jobs, confusing financial issues, and groceries. Elizabeth still feels a need to connect with her parents herself; she believes they will be lonely if she does not visit at night. There is also the very real concern that her mother is entering a stage of her disease in which she will be unable to remember Elizabeth. The child inside her does not want to miss the bits she can still receive from her mother. There is so much that is already gone; Elizabeth longs for the days when she could talk over a problem with her mom, unburden her daily frustrations, and share her successes. The best she can hope for these days is to sit next to her mom and look at old pictures or watch a television show. Her mother can no longer carry on a conversation and often does not understand simple sentences. While this creates great pain and feelings of loss for Elizabeth, she also finds that she is grateful that the process is slow and that she still has her mother in some form. Elizabeth does not want to miss a minute.

Elizabeth's husband also has living parents. They reside in another state but also require her husband's attention. Trips to visit create financial strain, and her husband will soon be helping to move his father to a nursing home. The emotional stress of these issues affects the family.

Between her children and her parents and in-laws, Elizabeth feels like she is running in circles. While most of the time she can manage to keep an even keel, there are moments when she feels as if she is going over the edge. It is usually some relatively small occurrence in the scope of her day that pushes her to the brink. In these moments, she uses self-talk to convince herself she can manage. She is aware of the paradoxical situation that she is caught in: She needs to see her counselor, but she does not have time! The thought of taking the time to get to the therapist's office and back makes her feel even more stressed, so she has canceled her recent appointments. Elizabeth wonders if her friends really understand her limited availability to spend time with them. She makes coffee dates and then cancels because something comes up or she is too tired.

Elizabeth knows that her current situation will have to change if she is to stay physically and emotionally healthy. She is aware that she and her husband do not spend enough time together and that they are both too exhausted for sex. She is bright enough to know that, if she cannot find 30 minutes to take a walk or time to get to her therapist, she needs to look closely at her life and make changes. She also does not like how she is becoming resentful and snappy at her family members, especially when she loses patience with her mother.

Elizabeth's life presents a model for how many midlife caregivers in the Sandwich Generation lose themselves. They are so busy trying to attend to the needs of everyone around them that their own needs suffer. Many individuals at midlife become so overwhelmed with all that they do that they develop physical illnesses or mental health concerns such as depression and anxiety.

This chapter uses the busy caregiver's life as a model to search out and describe ways for the caregiver to make time for herself. Embedded in this section is the Caregiver's Creed, which can be adapted to the needs of the individual. The how-to's of making moments for the self within each day are addressed, and a sample schedule is provided. Without these moments of self-care, the millions of women and men who are caregivers will not have time to experience moments of their own joy and happiness. This is the only life that you have. As you will see, it *is* possible to have a busy life and to make time for the self. In fact, it is crucial to make this time. It simply takes consciousness, perseverance, and good humor.

Please do take special note of the Caregiver's Creed. It also appears as Appendix B in this book, so an attractive copy can be made and posted where it will be seen regularly, as a reminder. Reread it often, whether that means putting it on a wall by the bathroom mirror to ponder while brushing your teeth or enclosing it in plastic and using waterproof tape to mount it inside the shower for review while waiting that wonderful couple of minutes as the hair conditioner works its magic before its rinse. Yes, we all multitask, but the creed can bring back a helpful and calming perspective—with its all-important reminders to take care of yourself—so be sure it does not end up tucked on a shelf, out of sight, out of mind.

TAFFY: BEING PULLED IN 20 DIRECTIONS

The kids need a ride to the store to pick up supplies for a school project; it is after dinner, and the table needs to be cleaned off and the laundry done. One of the elders needs assistance with changing into his bedclothes and washing up for the evening. The phone is ringing, and the caller ID indicates that it is a friend in need calling to talk about her divorce. Before dinner began, one of the kids noticed that the ceiling in the downstairs bathroom is leaking.

In the multigenerational family, a typical evening looks much like the picture painted in the previous paragraph. It is an image a lot like those spin art pictures we all knew and loved at fairs in our youth—a cacophony (a mess?) of dark and light streaks, splashes, and splotches, but when you stand back and consider it, the picture is somehow so beautiful.

Of course, there are unplanned elements, other considerations that occur at the same time as the usual routine of events. One of the kids or the parents may have a special problem that can include anything from an illness, missing medication, or lost homework or teeth (depending on the age of the family member) to an emotional issue that requires attention from the caregiver.

It has probably already been a long day for the primary caregiver, who may have a headache or be feeling tired from work. The caregiver knows that he has to rally because there is a massive amount to attend to before settling down for the evening. If the caregiver is lucky, he has an intact marriage, and many of the chores can be shared with his spouse or partner. If he is not as lucky, he is a single parent attempting to balance all of the same tasks on his own.

The typical caregiver is 57 years old, female, married, and employed outside the home. She can expect to spend as many years caring for a parent as for her children. Now about two million women are part of the Sandwich Generation, caring for both their parents and their children. It is more often women who are in this sandwiched role because they generally outlive men and are taught by their culture to be caregivers.[1]

The statistics may seem staggering; however, as the Baby Boomers hit middle age, these figures are likely to increase substantially. The elderly are living longer and remaining at home longer, thus requiring longer years of care.

Each individual has one life to live and has choices to make about how she will live it under the circumstances that surround her. While it may seem a hopeless matter to be able to manage all the necessary components of a multigenerational family *and* be happy, there are solutions that can make life easier. Many of the coping strategies in this book are repeated in a variety of ways and messages because they are important to learn and because, if they are applied, they actually work. It is sometimes easy to get caught in a "woe-is-me" mindset, which is not helpful for two reasons. The first reason that self-pity is unhelpful is that negativity does not change the situation and only depletes energy from the self. The second reason to stay away from the "woe-is-me" attitude is that it is catching, and the last thing an overburdened caregiver wants to be surrounded by is other negative, unhappy people!

Those in the caregiver role must beware of becoming a martyr. The martyr role is unpleasant for everyone; the individual winds himself into a human "doing machine" and gives off a self-sacrificing air that distances others. This role can take on a life of its own as the martyr complains and continues to engage in the behaviors he is complaining about rather than asking for help or attempting to gain mastery over his own life. Often, the martyr is not even aware that he creates his own circumstances and believes that, if he does not step in to take care of things, the world will collapse. He must first become conscious of his own actions and responsibilities toward himself; *then* he can begin to develop alternatives. Unfortunately, this role of martyrdom is popular with caregivers. When an individual believes he is the only one who can take care of things effectively, he can feel powerful. The nature of "giving" and "taking care of others" complicates the martyr phenomenon; this individual may believe that he is acting in the service of others, and asking for help or taking care of himself can seem to fly in the face of his empowered role. The caregiver must make conscious choices about how he will live his life. Even when one is pulled in 20 directions, the decision can be made to focus on oneself, abandon martyrdom, and move forward as a caregiver who also has the ability to fulfill one's own needs and happiness.

Staying positive can be challenging when one is in the trenches. It requires a great deal of self-talk to remember to breathe, find joy, and laugh. This search for happiness is one of the most important quests for an individual facing any set of challenging circumstances—and in any arena in life. Learning to see the glass as more than half full can be a gift that you can give to yourself, should you choose to make the effort. It is all about remembering to be positive. Remember to look up and see the beautiful nighttime sky or the first buds on the trees in spring. Remember that the moment you are in is the only moment you may have with that person in front of you; your loved one could be easily gone tomorrow. Remember to notice and praise small successes in yourself and in others and to catch the critical and self-debasing voices and change the internal messages from ones of despair to ones of hope.

It is all in your head. You can have a mind that is cluttered with thoughts about the insurmountable misery around you, or you can choose to shift your thinking to make each moment a gift rather than a task. The simple act of consciously being positive can help ease the load with dramatic success.

NURTURING OURSELVES

The Caregiver's Creed that follows is designed to be a living model for a successful *and* happy life as a caregiver. The tenets of the creed may seem difficult for the caregiver to swallow, as she is so used to putting everyone else's need in front of her own. At first, putting herself first or making time for herself and her partner may seem impossible. However, with consciousness and practice, the caregiver will come to understand that, if she is not happy and healthy, those around her will not be either. The old adage "If Momma ain't happy, then no one's happy" is actually quite true. There is a difference between being selfish and having a self. Initially, the caregiver may feel that she simply cannot consider putting some of the creed into action because it seems so selfish. The distinction is that the creed is designed to preserve the self, not to promote selfishness. When an individual keeps giving and giving, the emotional well runs dry, and there is little or nothing left to give. She may become bitter and resentful, and underneath all the saccharine sweetness is a passive-aggressive anger waiting to be unleashed. To become a healthy and well-balanced caregiver who does not harbor underlying resentment and rage, she must learn ways to full up her emotional well. The creed provides ways to fill the well so that there will be more to give back.

At the end of this chapter, you will have the opportunity to design your own sample schedule and, in the process, to try out and apply some of the tenets in the creed. You will be able to insert desired activities for filling up your own emotional well into your daily routine. Begin by imagining that the creed is possible.

THE CAREGIVER'S CREED

I HAVE CHOICE.

I can choose to take this day and be grateful for it, or I can choose to be miserable. My life is in my own hands. I will choose to notice my thoughts when they are negative and consciously change them to more positive ways of thinking. I will remember that I am in charge of my own life and emotions. I will remind myself that, if I make my negative thinking more positive, my behaviors will naturally shift to more loving ones, and I will feel less resentful.

I WILL PUT MYSELF FIRST.

I will not be able to care for others if I am physically or emotionally drained. I must recognize that I must put myself first. If I can do this, I will be much better equipped to love, care for, and support my family. I will allow myself to feel all my feelings, including guilt. I will notice the feelings and then still do what I need to do to take care of myself. I may feel an emotion such as guilt, but I do not need to let it rule how I function.

I WILL TAKE TIME FOR MYSELF AND MY PARTNER.

I can and will take time each day for myself and also for my partner. If the telephone rings and I see it is someone I want to talk to who will listen to *me*, I will pick up the phone. When I need a break, I will have an established break room or place and inform my family that I will be resting for a half-hour. I will remember to look up at the sky. I will buy myself a small gift. I will paint my toes. I will have a night out each week, and I will maintain exercise or a hobby that pleases me.

I will also remember to make time for my partner and let him know how important he is to me. I will do small things each day to show him I love him. I will write him a note, or send him a text message, or have a quiet cup of coffee with him. I will remember to acknowledge his presence and love.

I WILL ESTABLISH A ROUTINE.
This will decrease chaos and increase my feelings of mastery of my environment. I will know much of what I can expect during the day, who will do it, and when it will get done. This will help the whole family know when I am available or not, so I can feel less guilty.

I WILL ASK FOR HELP.
I will ask a loved one or friend for help/respite, and/or I will hire help, so I will get a break and not be so isolated or alone. I will call family meetings to ensure that everyone in the family pitches in, and I will teach my children to help their grandparents.

I CAN SAY YES, MAYBE, LATER, OR NO.
It is my job to protect myself. I will have many things that I am required to do; however, I will also have many opportunities to set boundaries. When I make the decision to do something, I will be as positive as I can because it was my decision and choice. I will practice saying no, setting limits, and protecting my own time.

I WILL PAY ATTENTION TO MY OWN FEELINGS AND NEEDS.
I will notice if I am beginning to feel overwhelmed and set a boundary before it gets out of hand. I will notice when I feel guilty and still do what I need to do to take care of myself. Feelings just *are*. I can notice my feelings and still move forward without getting pulled back into old traps. If my feelings become unmanageable and I feel out of control, I can get professional help.

I WILL REMIND MYSELF THAT THIS IS MY ONE LIFE TO LIVE.
When I need a reason to do something for myself, I will consciously remind myself that this is *my* life; it is not my parents' or my children's life, and I must be responsible for making myself happy. No one else can be in charge of my happiness.

The Caregiver's Creed is meant to be embellished by each individual for her own purposes. This creed is meant to be used by those in the Sandwich Generation to hold onto the self and further develop coping skills. Each individual can add specific tenets for herself that may be helpful to her unique situation. If there is a particular area in which an adult child has difficulty, she can add a tenet that can help to ease her burden. For example, a caregiver may have challenges leaving her work at the office; she may then choose to add a tenet to the creed that states that she will leave work at 5:00 P.M. each day and will not bring work home with her. The creed is meant to be a living action plan that reminds the caregiver that she is important and must care for herself first.

As noted, it may feel selfish for some to put themselves first and to nurture themselves. The reality, however, is that, unless one is well both physically and emotionally, one will not be able to take care of others. One will become physically exhausted and emotionally bereft, an emotional state that will lead to resentment and anger. While it may be difficult to put oneself first, make this an important tenet of the creed.

NURTURING OUR PARTNERS

Once the caregiver is able to focus some of the energy that has been spread on his family back to himself, he will be in a better position to remember that his partner has needs, too. When an adult child is responsible for multigenerational caregiving, it can be hard to see the forest for the trees. The caregiver self becomes lost in the forest, and the caregiver's partner may suffer and feel a great loss in their personal relationship. It is crucial for the caregiver to find balance. He must attend first to himself, then to his partner, and then to the needs of the family. The foundation of the primary relationship must be solid and nurtured for all to work most effectively. If there is strife in the primary relationship, this will create stress on the entire family system.

Imagine a pyramid, with the self at the bottom on the widest tier. Next, imagine the primary relationship as the middle tier, creating further stability for the pyramid. The top tier of the pyramid in this imagery holds the rest of the family system, including the children, elders, and family pets. If the foundation of the self and the primary relationship is out of kilter, then the top tier of the pyramid, composed of those who need help, will likely be unstable.

At first, this thinking may appear to be radical and, as discussed, selfish. However, it clearly makes sense that, if the foundation is not secure, then the structure will fall down. If one considers a multigenerational family and applies the same concept, one can see that without a sturdy foundation, the family will flounder.

As the caregiver rekindles her relationship with her partner, she will receive back some of the attention and love that she needs so badly. Love is a circular event: give to get, get to give. The notion of caring for oneself and one's partner may seem to be common sense. In a world that is overly busy with the needs of others, however, it is crucial to make this notion conscious and deliberate.

Establishing a routine can be especially helpful in creating a conscious, planned life that specifies time for the self and one's partner. The traditional Little Black Book that may once have been kept for entertainment purposes now has new purpose: self-preservation. A schedule can be designed that is fairly consistent and that will help the caregiver and those around him to have a fairly clear idea of what to expect each day. It is important to note, however, that every day can come with its own unique set of unplanned emergencies and chaos. One must expect that the set schedule will be interrupted. You may ask, "Then why keep a schedule if it is to be upset by unknown circumstances?" The reason to keep a schedule is so that there will be even the briefest illusion of consistency; this illusion sets the stage for it to become conscious reality. The schedule is a plan to follow, all the while knowing that unforeseen events can impact the planning. There is comfort in expectation even if it is interrupted. The interrupting event will be managed and the scheduled plan can be revisited with the comfort of knowing that the scene is already set in place for the remainder of the day. It sounds comforting, doesn't it?

A simple schedule works the best so that alterations can be made when necessary. Examples of daily routines for both a weekday and a weekend day follow, and at the end of this chapter, there is space for you to design your own personal schedule. The schedule is meant to be adapted to your individual needs and choices. Inserted in the schedule each day should be small ways in which you attend to your own emotional needs and fill up your own well. (Such self-care initiatives are italicized in the following schedules.) In this way, you will have more to give, be less resentful, and find yourself experiencing a more fulfilling life. You are encouraged to purchase a scheduling book in which you record your own planned daily, weekly, and monthly activities. The blank schedule pages in this chapter can be used to practice using that scheduling book. With a planner, the days will become more organized, and your daily schedule will read almost like a diary of your life. You will be able to look at your schedule and see just how often you have spent time on yourself and your partner, as well as on others. Keeping a planner from year to year will provide you with an "at-a-glance" view of your world, which can be powerful and instructive. If you look at your book and see that a week has passed without any self-care activities, this can be instructional. When you are starting to establish a routine, it may be important for you to write even the small things you do for yourself in your schedule. The act of writing the words "break time" in the schedule can be powerful. It can also be energizing to see a date night or an outing with friends written in the schedule for the end of the week. When you have an enjoyable event to look forward to, it will help you to rise above the rough patches and self-pity.

THE WEEKDAY SCHEDULE

5:30–6:30 Up and at 'Em

Always *get up early enough* in the morning to have a few minutes to *breathe and sit* with coffee, tea, and/or a significant other for a few minutes. These are the moments that frame the day, and *slowing down* in the morning is precedent for how the rest of the day will flow. The morning shower can provide a good 10 minutes of freedom during which you can *say thanks* for all that is good in life and *find gratefulness* for the small things. The exercise of being grateful helps you to look at what is positive rather than focusing on the challenges of the upcoming day and, again, helps to set a foundation for a good day. A *quick review of the day* can also be done in the shower, which creates a focused map of how the day will proceed. Recalling the schedule for the day can be comforting when you know what will be likely to occur and in what order. Coffee, showering, and dressing generally require a half-hour. This timeframe intentionally leaves another *30 minutes of free time*. You may decide to use your 30 minutes before showering to *stretch and exercise*, or you may decide to use your extra time to *sleep a little longer*. The key to the first minutes of the morning is to *slow down, be grateful*, and *sit quietly with a partner and/or coffee*.

6:30–7:15 Breakfast and Kisses

Get the kids up. It will take children age six and up about 20 minutes to get dressed, make their beds, and wash up. A bit of coaching and mediating may be necessary if there is more than one child, but you can prepare breakfast during this time, watch the news, or read the paper. Then *shut off the television* and have everyone sit together for 15 minutes at the table for breakfast. Make one breakfast meal for all. It can be an error to be a short-order cook in a busy household. The kids will come to know that breakfast begins at a certain time and that they are expected to be at the table dressed and washed. It can also be helpful for the children to know the "breakfast of the day." For example, Mondays may be muffin day, Tuesdays could be eggs and toast, and so on. Once again, this establishes a specific schedule and creates expectation. You may even find that the morning rituals continue into your children's adult lives when they leave the nest. Beginning the day with an easy sit-down meal together is a warm and healthy way to establish relationships with your children that will guide them throughout their lives. Each person at the table should clean up her own plate and put her breakfast utensils in the dishwasher. Once everything is cleared, set the table for dinner. As the children get older, this can be one of their chores. It may seem ridiculous to set the table for dinner at 6:30 in the morning, but it only takes a few seconds, and you will be grateful that it is done tonight! Turn on the crock-pot if that is the meal for the evening, or leave a note for your teen to put the prepared chicken dish in the oven at a set time when he gets home from school. End your morning breakfast with the *ritual of a kiss or hug*. Your partner/spouse, the children, and even the pets are warm and loving receptacles for affection. If they are not available or if the morning has gotten off to a rocky start, *hug yourself*. No one will know what you are doing, and it will feel good. There is almost nothing like a good embracing self-hug! If there are elders in the home, they likely will sleep past the time of everyone's departure. Breakfast can be left for them on a warming plate with a short loving note. If there is a home help aide who comes in, this routine will have been established, and the elder will know what to expect during the day.

7:15 Out the Door
The car is your palace. With any luck, it is yours and yours alone. Even if you share the car with your spouse, you can develop rituals that make your time traveling a positive experience that continues to frame the way your day begins. If you travel with your partner, you may choose to use this time to chat about the children, the elders, your work, or plans for entertainment for just the two of you. The car may provide some of the *quiet moments* that you and your spouse can have difficulty finding elsewhere in your day. If you travel alone, these may be some of your few moments of true aloneness and privacy. Some individuals may choose to listen to the news on the radio or their own music or to talk to a friend via car speakerphone. You may also choose to ride in quiet, enjoying the route and the solitude of the drive.

7:45 At the Office
Nest in at the office a bit before almost everyone else gets there. There will likely be some other wise office mate who knows that settling in early at work makes the day a bit easier, so be prepared that you may not be alone.

Use the first minutes at work to get your coffee, look at messages, and listen to voice mail. These early moments begin the day at a lovely pace, and once your "real" day begins, it will seem much more manageable.

8:00–10:30 Work
10:30–10:45 *Break*
Do a bit of personal business, make a phone call to check on your elder, *breathe, stretch, step outside for some air, drink a glass of water,* or *have a snack.*

10:45–12:00 Work
12:00–1:00 *Lunch*
Eat. Do not skip food. This is the fuel your body needs to function, both physically and mentally. A small meal is fine, and if you can, *get outside or eat with a friend* or coworker. This social ritual is also a good one to develop. The opportunity to *talk with others* about your life is healthy and provides perspective on your life dilemmas. Make a brief check-in call to the elders during this time if needed.

1:00–2:45 Work
2:45–3:00 *Break*
There are some offices that do not schedule breaks for their employees. If this is the case, it is then your responsibility to find ways to take 15-minute breathers at your desk. A stash of snacks can be kept in your desk drawer, and a form of quiet meditation can be accomplished without anyone realizing the "shop has been closed" for a few minutes. Make sure you take care of yourself. It is unlikely that anyone else will be watching out for you, and success is measured by sharpness, not droopy, resentful employees!

3:00–5:00 Work
And along comes the most challenging part of the day: the evening. The onslaught of the next few hours can be the most demanding and overwhelming; therefore, a schedule for the evening hours can be the most useful tool of the caregiver. Establish your routine so that it works for you! A sample model will be provided, but there will also be the expected changes that accompany parenthood: a child's concerts, sports events, parent/teacher conferences, and a variety of other events that will impinge upon the established routine. Take heart! The routine will help you master the colliding extracurricular activities.

5:00–5:30 The Palace

You are now back in the car, your palace, heading home. Use the time to *shrug off the workday and leave it behind you.* Work will be there in the morning when you return, and ruminating on what was said or what was or was not done or on the boss will not change the circumstances. Remind yourself that the office is work, not life. And you are now headed to life and the important part of your existence. When individuals cannot make the shift from the office to home, they will be caught in a place that is in between; family members will not get what they need, and neither will you. Mastering the task of being in the moment at home and leaving work behind sometimes takes a conscious act. If there was an event at work that feels unfinished, it can become consuming and affect the attention that is needed for life at home. Shrug it off and remind yourself that you want to *be present and in the moment.* You may find you need to remind yourself of this several times as the thoughts about work creep back in to interfere with home life. If, indeed, there is something critical from work that needs attention in the evening, plan to allow 30 minutes after the children are settled to take care of this business. However, make this kind of situation the exception to the rule. The rule is that work will remain at work. There are times when rules can be broken but not without using good judgment. How important is it that the task be completed at home? Use your wisdom to manage your priorities. If you make the conscious decision that some work needs to be done at home, keep it contained to as limited a time as possible. *Shake it off!*

5:30–6:00 Back into the Looking Glass

The kids are picked up from after-school care or have come home on the bus, so once you exit from your palace, it is a time of full-force energy. As you enter your home, *take a precious 10 minutes to breathe, unwind, and change into comfortable clothes.* Tell the kids and the elders that you need 10 minutes to undress and unwind and then you will be with them. As you are shedding your office outfit, *stretch, and remind yourself to pace your evening.* It will all get done.

6:00–7:30 Dinner Hour

The table was set in the morning. The meal was planned over the weekend, so you know just what is going in the oven or coming out of the crock-pot. Perhaps one of the teens was home early enough to have put the chicken in the oven, or you or your spouse is cooking on the grill. You have time here, if you have planned ahead (see the weekend schedule coming up in the next section), to check in with the kids about their day and homework or to spend some time with your elders, who will likely want to recite their daily activities to you even if it was just watching television or doing the laundry. Remind yourself to be attentive. *Sit close and remember to touch your loved one.* This will fill your emotional well, too. These moments can be your time for intimacy in a busy day, so capture them; they are fleeting, and there will be no return to that last minute that just passed. Dinner is soon ready and apt to be a noisy event in a blended family. Have an *arranged dinner time*, and try to stick to it unless there is an outside family event that interferes. If everyone knows that dinner is served at 6:30, all family members will know to schedule their own activities around dinner. As teens get older, some of them will have work schedules or activities that keep them from the sit-down dinner, but everyone else who is available can attend. An elder may require extra help with knowing the time, getting to the table, and eating. The role reversal that has been previously discussed may become evident as the grandparents' meat may have to be cut for them, and they may need to be cued to eat and take their evening medications. If the family has two adult children, one can take the role of attending to the elderly parents while the other sets out the food, monitors young children, and orchestrates the cleanup. If the family has only one adult caregiver, these tasks will need to be juggled, and teenagers can be coached to help. Dinner can be a lively and loving event, with stories shared from the day and from the past along with plans for future events. The mealtime can fly by. The matter of actually eating may take only 30 minutes; however, on a good day, family members will *linger* and spend time talking. Cleanup is *shared*. Children and teens should have their own responsibilities for helping in the aftermath of dinner. They can clear the table, stack dishes, and wipe counters while the caregiver assists the elder with changing into her nightwear, removing and brushing teeth, and washing up. The after-dinner ritual of helping one's elderly parent can be an intimate time. The elder may need help remembering even small details or may physically need assistance in changing. She may have been alone for most of the day, so she will be craving attention and touch. The caregiver may be tired from the day, but these moments and opportunities will not be there forever, so it is important to remember to make the most of the time there is. Patience is an act of love; repeating the same direction 10 times or coaching the same activity again and again may be frustrating; however, it is often a new way of communicating to an elder loved one. *Staying in the moment* with the elder and being loving and playful are a way to create joint meaning. The elder may forget details or at times even who the caregiver is, but she will remember the feelings that accompany the interaction.

7:30–8:30 Family Games, Homework, and Time for the Elders
If the children are still young, the ritual of a family game is often a wonderful time to *laugh* together. This is a time that the children of the family really enjoy and request once it is an established routine. Each family member has a night to choose the game and set it up. The actual game playing usually lasts less than 30 minutes, but it is an opportunity to laugh together. After the game, the children clean up and go to the kitchen table for 30 minutes of assisted homework. As the children become teenagers, after dinner they will move into their own rooms with their homework, iPods, and computers, and the caregiver will be free to spend the hour with the elders. Many elders are happy simply having the adult caregiver in the same room with them watching a television show. Others will want to talk or play a card game or even have a glass of cream sherry.

8:30–9:00 Prepare for Tomorrow
This is the wind-down time that leads to the best part of the evening. The younger children are tucked in, and a short story or prayer is read. Words of praise for some accomplished task or wonderful personality trait are shared each day with each child. This is another of those moments of intimacy and fortification for your children that will have long-reaching positive effects. As children fall asleep, they will hear just how much they are esteemed and loved. Teenagers are told how they are loved and reminded to keep it down. Clothes for the next day are set out so the morning will be breezy. The outfits can be jazzed up for fun or dressed down for a more relaxed day. Lunches are made, and they can inspire a creative flair. Spice them up with a treat, or tuck a note in a lunch bag that someone will find the next day.

9:00 *Woo-hoo Time*
Finally! As the day comes to a close, this is *your time*—no more work, no more caregiving, no further responsibilities until the next morning. There is so much to do for the self and so little time left! *Read a book, watch a television show or movie, spend time with your partner, make a telephone call to a friend, dabble on the Internet. Ahhh, the possibilities!* And, of course, tumble into bed and sleep until the next day dawns. While it may be tempting to stay up until all hours to experience these moments of freedom, it is

also a good thing to establish a routine bedtime (sorry). In general, a solid eight hours of sleep is a good rule of thumb. (Women may need a bit more, men a bit less.) However, you have done so well with your day that you may want to *reward yourself* with a little extra time and spend an extra hour in a relaxing activity. Enjoy!

THE WEEKEND SCHEDULE

This schedule is going to cheer you up considerably. The weekend can be a much *less structured time*. In fact, it is suggested that weekends can be primarily unstructured, except for a few tasks on Sundays that will help to prepare for the weekday schedule. After a full five days with a schedule that continually predicts the next thing to be done, it is important to have two days of the week that can be adapted at will to the *whims and needs of the self* and the family. Three constants are recommended, however. The first is to maintain the dinner schedule so children, teens, and elders know that they can expect this one consistent time every night to gather together. The caregiver can mix this up a bit by suggesting that the family go out to eat or that they get an easy meal delivered, such as pizza or sandwiches. Any family tradition can be developed for Saturday nights, such as pizza delivery and a movie that all can watch. The second recommendation for routine is that on Sunday afternoons meals be planned and prepared for the following week. When this is done ahead of time, it makes the weekday madness much easier to manage. The third weekend recommendation is to *plan time each weekend for an enjoyable activity*. This can be a family activity, *a night out with one's partner*, or *an outing with friends*. It can sometimes help for the caregiver to *clearly state a time that he reserves for his own activities* so that will become the family's expectation. The caregiver *may decide that he will reserve every Friday night for his own pleasure*. Once this plan is in place, if necessary, home help can be brought in for several hours on Friday nights to feed and care for the children and elders. If supervision is not yet necessary for the grandparents, a meal can be brought in for the elders and children. Nightwear can be laid out, and the caregivers are free for an entire evening. *Couples should plan on having a date night at least twice a month, and the remaining two Fridays can be used however the caregiver chooses to please himself.*

Each individual's schedule will need to be personalized to address her own wants and needs, including events that will serve to fill her emotional well. Some schedules may have events such as weekly or monthly massages, scheduled musical entertainment, sports events, time for the beach, girls' nights out, book club meetings, hobbies, or any other variety of activities that may be of interest to the caregiver. It can be challenging at first for some caregivers to even know what they might like to do for themselves; this is not especially unusual. The caregiver role can be one that may have begun years before the move into the Sandwich Generation. This role of focusing on others may have solidified over time. While it may feel easy for the caregiver to know what to do for others, even when exhausted, she may have great difficulty knowing what to do for herself.

It may be helpful for the adult child to make a wish list of all the activities that he has enjoyed in the past or has wished that he had time for in the present. There is a workspace included at the end of this chapter for you to begin to develop your own set of wishes. The list may include major events, such as a much-desired trip to Hawaii, and also should include lots of smaller items, such as playing a round of golf, reading a good book, enjoying a night away, having time to read the daily newspaper, doing some personal shopping (new shoes, a coat, etc.), or getting a manicure. Once the list is developed, the small items can be inserted into the daily or weekly schedule. The larger events, such as the trip to Hawaii or costly entertainment tickets, can be set as goals for the future. The expense of the event will help determine how far ahead it will need to be planned. Any and all wishes and dreams need to be put in writing on the list. It is all possible. The only requirements are an open mind and a plan.

ASKING FOR HELP

The final recommendation in this chapter for improving quality of life for the caregiver is to begin asking for help. Once again, the caregiver may find him in foreign waters. There is some likelihood that the adult child has not been in the habit of asking for assistance from others and does not know where or how to begin a quest for help. In some circumstances, the caregiver may not be aware that he needs help until he is so completely overwhelmed that the situation has become a crisis. At this point, it can become much harder to ask for assistance.

While the concept of asking for help from others can be daunting in itself, there can be other reasons caregivers do not ask for assistance. It may feel as though it is easier to just do the task oneself than to try to find the words or courage to ask for help. The individual may not know how to make requests and can fear rejection.

Some Sandwich Generation caregivers may have built their entire personal code on doing everything for everybody else. If they admit, even to themselves, that they need help, it may feel like a character flaw. Personality traits, such as overidentifying with the role of caregiver, can be a considerable obstacle to overcome in the process of asking for help. If one believes that it is one's role in life to be a caregiver and one suddenly needs help, how can one justify this need to oneself?

Individuals who need assistance can mistakenly assume that, if they request help, they may seem incompetent or weak to others. Some people spend their lives attempting to show the world that they are self-sufficient, even to the extent of personal collapse. It can be extraordinarily difficult to shift out of a pattern of caregiving and ask for help if one has a core belief that it is one's duty to care for others. These core beliefs are generally instilled during childhood and can be challenging to change. Once they are identified, however, core beliefs can be altered by conscious intent to change. It can be helpful for the caregiver to remember that highly successful people make it a habit to ask for help. The successful person knows her own strengths and weaknesses, knows how to delegate, and knows when to ask for help.

Learning to ask for and accept help is a marvelous way for the caregiver to fill his emotional well. Obtaining help will not mean that all control is being surrendered or that the caregiver's family will be taken away. It simply means that the caregiver is taking a respite, sitting back for a few brief moments to regroup, and allowing someone else to be the driver for a short period.

No one likes to impose on another, and this is yet another reason it may be difficult to request assistance. It is important to remember that, when help is requested, it accomplishes several things. The first, and most crucial for this exercise, is that asking for help can provide an opportunity for relief for the caregiver. Several other secondary gains can be reaped from the request for help. The person who is asked will feel needed, the caregiver will feel less isolated, intimacy will be built between the person asked and the caregiver, and the recipient of the help will likely benefit from having a "fresh" helper.

While the caregiver may develop a feeling of indebtedness toward the helper, it is important to note that favors can be returned. The helper may have a different need that the caregiver can fulfill, which would give the adult child a break from her routine and provide a fresh outlook. The cycle of asking for help and being helped can be powerfully rewarding, and a support network can grow out of one simple request.

It is not the responsibility of the caregiver to do the work for everyone, including trying to figure out if a potential helper will be willing or available. When the caregiver does not ask for assistance, he may rob the helper of an opportunity to say yes and to be more fully present in the adult child's world. The helper may have witnessed the caregiver struggling and want to be of assistance but fear intruding. When a person asks for help, he begins a dialogue that can lead to deeper shared relationships. There may be times when the person who is asked for help says no; this can also create a shared understanding. The reasons for the refusal may help the caregiver develop a wider worldview in which he is not the only one overwhelmed by life's tasks.

The concern that, if someone else takes over the job, it will not get done correctly can also impede the caregiver from requesting the help needed. The reality is that the job will certainly be done differently if someone else is doing it; however, unless there are safety issues, the differences in care will not have long-term adverse affects. The caregiver must learn to let go of high standards and the belief that her own care ideals are the only ones that are acceptable. She may find that there are alternative ways of caregiving that can work well; with outside help, both caregiver and elder will likely experience a renewed happiness in being together. The harried adult child who is caring for a demented parent and two acting-out teenagers will certainly be better equipped to show affection to family members after a respite. The teens and the parent with dementia will likely reap benefits from the break, as well, and be more inclined to have close feelings for the caregiver upon that person's return. Secondary gains could include the caregiver's learning new ways to work with dementia or to parent rebellious teenagers from the helper.

With each concern that arises regarding the need for assistance, there emerges a greater benefit. While the process of requesting help may be uncomfortable and new, it becomes easier each time it is done. There are also resources in the community that can be accessed by the caregiver. The church and its members can be a wonderful source of support for respite care. There are also other community supports available for those who have financial resources. The act of paying a helper to come in twice a month to clean the house or do the laundry can be of tremendous help to the caregiver, both physically and emotionally. Neighborhood teens can be paid to do shoveling in the winter or run errands; respite care can be paid for from community sources.

Help is available. The task is to reach out.

Personalized Care Schedule

5:00 A.M.–6:00 A.M.

_____

_____

_____

_____

_____

6:00 A.M.–7:00 A.M.

_____

_____

_____

_____

_____

7:00 A.M.–8:00 A.M.

_____

_____

_____

_____

_____

8:00 A.M.–9:00 A.M.

_____

_____

_____

_____

_____

9:00 A.M.–10:00 A.M.

_____

_____

_____

_____

_____

10:00 A.M.–11:00 A.M.

_____

_____

_____

_____

_____

Personalized Care Schedule (Continued)

11:00 A.M.–12:00 P.M.

_____

_____

_____

_____

_____

12:00 P.M.–1:00 P.M.

_____

_____

_____

_____

_____

1:00 P.M.–2:00 P.M.

_____

_____

_____

_____

_____

2:00 P.M.–3:00 P.M.

_____

_____

_____

_____

_____

3:00 P.M.–4:00 P.M.

_____

_____

_____

_____

_____

4:00 P.M.–5:00 P.M.

_____

_____

_____

_____

_____

(*Continued*)

(Continued)

5:00 P.M.–6:00 P.M.

6:00 P.M.–7:00 P.M.

7:00 P.M.–8:00 P.M.

8:00 P.M.–9:00 P.M.

9:00 P.M.

WISH LIST

SIX

Finances

Clara digs farther into her purse. She is quite sure she tucked a $20 bill into her side compartment. Clara always keeps a small "extra bill" in her pocketbook for times that she runs out of cash. She feels ridiculous going through her personal items looking for money as she holds up other people at the cashier line. She finally decides she had better use her credit card or someone behind her is going to get hostile.

As Clara walks to her car, she wonders if one of her teens has pilfered her purse again. Her kids are aware that she stuffs extra bills in nooks and crannies for "emergencies." Clara is very generous with them, but her big heart does not include allowing them to go through her personal items for quick cash. She is not their bank. She feels anger that one of her children would fail to respect her boundary this way and intends to speak with the family about private space at dinner.

Clara sighs as she realizes that money is becoming an issue that needs attention within the family. Her teenagers are at the stage where they want the fashion jeans that cost an exorbitant $80 a pair and they have little concept of their parents' financial status. The family has never lacked much; while they are not wealthy, they are able to keep up with the middle-class needs of their children.

At midlife, Clara and her husband, Peter, like to think they can have a car that works reliably and that, if one of their major appliances needs replacement, they can afford this without a bank loan. The couple also feels good that they are able to take a family vacation for a week each year and manage one or two couples weekends for themselves. Clara's husband has always wanted a Harley-Davidson motorcycle, and although Clara cannot quite understand this, she wants her husband to be able to make this purchase. Clara can see that, if Peter does not buy the Harley now, he will soon be past the age of truly being able to enjoy it. A motorcycle does not seem like much to ask for after a full life of work, and Clara is determined that they will make this purchase.

There are other upcoming financial issues to consider. Their three children are quite bright and are all headed to college. Tuitions are going up along with the cost of living for everything else. There are relatively small savings accounts in each teenager's name, marked for college. These funds will likely only partially help with the first year at the local state college. At least one of the children has aspirations of going to a prestigious college out of state.

Clara and Peter hope to retire before they turn 90, a plan that is not looking all that good at the moment. They have been thoughtful about their retirement planning, and each has a decent savings account, but with the recent downturn of the market, they have lost more than a third of their saved money. It is looking as if they will need to keep working well past age 62. Even with extending their work years, they will now reap only enough from their Social Security benefits to maintain a meager retirement. They are also quite worried about the rumors that Social Security monies are going to dry up before it is their turn to retire. Peter has some health issues that complicate his remaining at work for many more years, and Clara worries about his condition worsening over time.

In the last several years, their family has begun to support Peter's mother financially, as well. While she receives a small pension check from her deceased husband's employer, it is barely enough to cover her rent. Peter and Clara subsidize his mother by paying for her utilities, groceries, and many other miscellaneous needs, such as snow shoveling and home care.

Each month Clara sits with the bills, and each month they seem to mysteriously grow. Clara is aware that her teens need to be coached in family finances and how they work; she needs to make the time to sit with them and include them in the family financial planning. She does not want them to be worried, but she does want to teach them about being conservative with their demands and making sustainable purchases that will last them and be good for the environment.

Clara is fairly frugal herself, but when she feels like she needs or wants something, she buys it for herself. She shops at Walmart, a choice that drives Peter crazy. He wants Clara to have finer things, but Clara is content with her purchases, and she gets much more for her money at discount stores.

She has always been able to make the money work. When Clara and Peter were a young couple just starting out, Clara took pride in both paying all the bills and squirreling money away for pizza or a movie once a week. When the children were young, money was tight, but there had always been enough for extra activities and new winter boots. Suddenly, with college and Peter and Clara's desired retirement looming ahead, she wonders if they are going to be able to survive.

Clara angrily feels as if she is being cheated. She and Peter have worked hard all their lives, lived reasonably, saved as much money as they could, and paid their high taxes every year. Now, at this late stage in her life, Clara does not think she can find any way possible to buy Peter his long-awaited motorcycle. Worse than that, Clara wonders if they will be able to keep the pantry full once they are finally able to retire.

Clara finds herself shaking her head in the parking lot of the grocery store. She reminds herself to "shake it off" and not to panic. She trusts herself, and Peter, to design a financial plan that will help them avoid poverty and living in the streets during their golden years. She decides that "The New Financial Plan" will begin tonight with a family conversation about the sacredness of her purse. It will be the metaphor that she can use for how the family needs to think about their resources. Clara gathers her well-developed midlife wits about her and proceeds in the direction that she needs to go to make her life "good enough."

THE NEW FINANCIAL PLAN

The conscious awakening to the need for a plan is the first step in the creation of a map that will provide direction. The midlife individual must realize that she needs a new way to look at her finances once she becomes part of the Sandwich Generation. Caring for both one's children and one's parents will generally include a financial component. Lucky sandwiched adults may have wealthy elders who can lavish upon them all the financial resources necessary for their care. Some elders may not be wealthy but can contribute financially to the extended family, money that can also help tremendously. However, many of those in the Sandwich Generation will be fully responsible for the care of their parents without much financial compensation. The sooner the realization that finances may be strained dawns on the midlife individual, the sooner a plan can be drafted to meet the developing needs of the family system. This plan can provide a vision for the financial future, which in turn may create a feeling of some control that can be helpful in maintaining composure under duress. Much like the Caregiver's Creed and the daily schedule that the sandwiched individual develops, the financial plan creates a road map. Rather than being lost in feelings of anger and helplessness, the caregiver has a map that provides goals and a path to follow.

The plan can include some basic features and concepts that will be addressed in this chapter for consideration. Like the previous chapter on the self, this chapter will emphasize the ever-important concept of putting oneself first. The individual or couple should be sure that their own financial needs are secure before attempting to manage the monetary needs of others. Dave Ramsey, financial planner, has a general piece advice for those who are caring for children and aging parents. He states, "Only the strong can help the weak, so your first goal must be to get yourself financially under control."[1] It is important for the midlife individual to be not only physically and emotionally stable but financially stable as well. Ramsey goes on to state that "you are the goose, and if you kill the goose, there will be no more golden eggs. Taking care of your financial needs first is not selfish, it's smart."[2]

How does an individual or couple put themselves first financially? There are several rules of thumb that can be followed in the quest to maintain financial solvency when facing multiplying needs. Many of them are simple common sense.

Keep savings accounts sacred. Midlife people have worked hard, and many have established the savings of half a lifetime. These savings have come with sacrifice, fortitude, and foresight. Now is not the time to give up on the vision! The only savings that should be dipped into are those that were wisely set aside for college or elder care. Many of those in midlife will not have generated specific accounts for these circumstances, but that does not mean that the savings that has been accumulated for other causes such as retirement should be pilfered. It makes no good sense to rob from Peter to pay Paul. Do not dip into retirement savings, even if it is tempting to do so, unless there is a crisis. "Don't sabotage your own financial future to take care of a parent—you don't want this vicious cycle to affect your children" (p. 3).[3]

As challenging as it may seem, continue to save money despite family obligations.[4] It can be most helpful to have a set amount of money from one's paycheck deposited directly in a savings account each pay period. The direct deposit method of savings can remove some of the easy access that can contribute to using money for other purposes. While the impulse may be there to use funds for one's children or elders, additional effort is then needed to take money out of the bank that has already been deposited.

Money that is directly deposited into savings seems more invisible: out of sight, out of mind.

Caregivers who work outside of the home need to "take advantage of employer-provided accounts, at least up to the point of matching contributions. Be sure to max out on a traditional deductible IRA or Roth IRA if you are eligible, or a small business retirement plan if you are self-employed. Put excess savings into your brokerage account. Then manage the whole thing from the top down with a tax-efficient asset-allocation plan based on your risk tolerance and time horizon."[5]

Develop a budget and stick to it. Make the budget realistic, based upon what money is brought in and the necessities of the household. Be sure to include a budget line for self-care, even if it is small. Going to the movies or out to dinner once or twice a month is important in the larger scheme of things, so even if it is tempting to leave this out of the budget, put it in.

One needs to be specific as one is developing a budget. One should sit down with pen and paper or a computer spreadsheet and evaluate the amount of money that is brought into the household. The next step is to formulate just what portion of the money is used for monthly bills, such as rent, mortgage, electricity, water, food, and gas. These figures are deducted from the money that has been brought in. There will likely be money remaining, and the individual who has never budgeted before may be surprised to see just how much is left. The remaining monies can be used for self-care, kids' allowances, toiletries for the elders, and home help.

The creation of this budget will be a valuable exercise and will once again create some feeling of mastery and control. Knowing what one has in one's accounts, what will go out for the basic needs of the family, and what is left over can help to determine planning needs. Information and clarity can be gained from educating oneself regarding one's household financial status. From the information gathered, the caregiver can realistically see what can be accomplished and what may need to be eliminated.

It is also recommended that open conversations occur among family members regarding finances.[6] Once a budget has been developed, clear conversations can begin regarding the family financial needs and how each member can contribute. Children at all ages can be a part of these dialogues. It may be a good idea to begin family meetings early in the life of the family, and then they will be an expected family ritual. Family meetings can be called by any family member and can be used to celebrate a success or discuss an event that needs clarification. These meetings can also be used to make plans for the family in terms of weekend outings or changes in schedules, chores, and routines. These meetings provide the time to clarify family dynamics and address issues that arise. It is important to strike a balance in the family meeting and to be sure to use some of the meeting time to celebrate good deeds, grades, and other praiseworthy circumstances. If family meetings have been a routine exercise for the family, it will be an easy move to use this arena to talk about general money issues. Otherwise, instituting the first family meeting may initially feel awkward. Once it has been established that the family will meet routinely, it will come to be expected, and many times family members will look forward to this time to talk together.

The first time the family meets ground rules need to be established. They can be simple rules, such as not interrupting each other, staying in the room when others are talking, and not watching television or listening to iPods or texting when the family is together. Meetings can be as short or as long as needed, and whoever initiates the meeting may need to remind members of the rules. Excitement can be generated at these meetings, and everyone may want to talk at once, so the reminder to listen politely without interrupting is critical for the meeting to be effective. Some families have a token they pass; the person holding the token has the floor and passes it when he is finished speaking. The token can be any meaningful object for the family—a special stone, a carved stick, or any object that marks the leadership for the moment.

Talking about money can be uncomfortable, especially if family members are not used to meeting together and have never had monetary discussions. It may be helpful to have the first few family meetings about other subjects, such as house rules, changes in chores, and plans for a celebration or family outing. As family members become oriented to what it is like to have a family meeting, they will become more comfortable sitting together to have discussions and solve problems. They will be more easily able to move into more challenging conversations, such as those about finances.

It may be helpful for the caregiver who initiates the meeting about finances to think about that conversation as she does about any other discussion. Money issues can be intimidating and can be laced with many levels of meaning. The caregiver may be hesitant to bring up financial issues because she is concerned her parents may think she is asking for help. Elderly parents may expect a great deal of privacy around their financial status because of the way that they were raised; therefore, their midlife caregivers can be uncomfortable raising questions. Because of all of the taboos surrounding money, it can be important to normalize this conversation, keeping the subject light and the first meeting regarding this subject short. Individual follow-up meetings can be held with elders so they do not feel so exposed in a group in terms of divulging what they may consider personal financial information.

The initial family meeting regarding finances simply begins the conversation and can be direct and straightforward. The primary caregivers may simply want to say that they have developed a budget and inform the family of any changes that may result from this new plan. Caregivers will want to remove any excessive worry from children and elders about financial survival prospects. They will also want to help the family understand that the new world economy and additional family responsibilities make it necessary for everyone to pay attention to the newly established budget. At this meeting, any changes as a result of financial issues can be announced, such as longer working hours or cutbacks to be at home more. "The sandwich situation calls for open interfamily conversations to help ensure that money is managed thoughtfully and effectively, as well as cooperatively."[7]

Money may be a sensitive subject, but good things can happen when families discuss finances. "It's important to have the conversation in an open, nonjudgmental way. While finances are a taboo subject for many reasons, harmony can be realized through understanding and communication. In some cases, families may find it helpful to include a neutral third party, such as a financial advisor, to act as a facilitator" (p. 2).[8]

A financial advisor can be instrumental in helping families to develop an action plan that prepares them for their current living arrangements and for the future. Advisors are savvy in their advice and may suggest that an elder law attorney become involved to protect any assets the family would like to preserve. The costs of this may seem prohibitive, but the long-term rewards make the investment in an advisor and an attorney worthwhile. Elder law attorneys may suggest the movement of assets, guardianship, and other protective means to preserve funds.

If the elders are residing in the home as part of the extended family, they may be able to contribute financially to the household needs. The elders can also have determined tasks around the home that can help to make them feel useful and provide some relief for the caregiver. These tasks will need to be based on the level of functioning of the elder. For example, some tasks might include gardening, doing laundry, and caring for animals left at home during the day. In the same respect, once children reach majority and still remain living at home, it is important for them to contribute in some way to the collective family. Children who have grown to majority should have their own clear financial plan designed in conjunction with their parents. This plan may include payment of a set amount of rent, payment of a portion of utilities, or other financial arrangement. It is also a good idea to have children at any age begin to contribute small portions of their money to their own college savings, such as the 529 College Plan or other accounts.[9] Parents can set up accounts for their children and discuss depositing portions of money they receive for holidays, for birthdays, and from part-time jobs. While it may seem stern to require young adults to contribute financially to the home or to savings, it is an excellent teaching tool for their own financial futures. These youngsters are soon to be launched into the world, and preparing them to be responsible financially while still in the nest is part of parenting. Young adults remaining at home should also have a share of the other household responsibilities. They need to share in the chores, such as preparing dinner two or three nights a week, spending time with their elders, or doing laundry or other needed tasks. It is important for parents and young adults to set up an agreement covering financial and shared responsibilities so that there is no confusion and each person knows what is expected. This agreement will help the family unit to work more smoothly with fewer burdens placed on the caregiver.

Family meetings can be used to review how assigned daily tasks are working and whether alterations need to be made due to a change of circumstances. Commenting on a deliciously cooked dinner or how beautiful the garden looks can go a long way at these meetings. Praising family members in front of each other has a power of reinforcement that is strong. If one child has been able to sock a great deal of money into his savings, let the family know! The child will feel acknowledged for his hard work and want to put even more money away.

It is also important to recognize that many of these suggestions for planning and financial savings are designed for the middle class—for people who are privileged, hold jobs, and have some assets. Many underprivileged and struggling minority groups do not have the same secure middle-class living arrangements as the majority. Midlife members of these underrepresented populations may need assistance from the county or state and have to find alternative ways of financial survival as they are sandwiched between elders and growing children. Unfortunately, the growing children of these underrepresented groups often experience the reality that government service, as in the armed services, is the only way to eventually be able to obtain a college education. Savings accounts are a dream, as life is lived day to day in the hope for meals and shelter. These groups may struggle financially, but many have learned from hardship to stick together. For many in the minority, the idea of the blended, extended family system is not foreign. Sharing resources, space, and food may be the way they have always lived. Conversely, for those in the majority

who have lived most of their lives in a smaller nuclear family, the concept
of a larger living system can be novel and overwhelming.

Underrepresented multicultural groups have long been good at supporting their group members and surviving. They may find the Sandwich Generation a comfortable concept, as the collective way of living and sharing
may be familiar to them. Community and government resources can aug-
ment the needs of these groups as they continue to support their families
within their cultural systems.

ONE PIECE OF THE PIE

An individual's life can be thought of as a pie with many slices that
make up the whole. Each piece of the pie is dependent upon the others
to make up the whole pie. The slices need to be relatively balanced in size
to keep the pie in its natural shape. Each piece is interdependent on the
others to maintain the balance. When one piece of pie is removed, the rest
of the pie dribbles down into the empty slot, making the remainder of the
pie lopsided and unappealing to look at. Sometimes the remaining pieces
of pie can manage to stand tall, but once still other pieces are removed,
the shape and distinction of the pie are lost.

In each life, there are many important pieces that make up the whole.
They can be thought of like pie slices. Each slice represents an important
part of the self. There will be universal slices in each person's pie, and
there will also be slices unique to that specific individual's personality.
Some fairly universal slices may include health/well-being, home, family,
work, finances, and relationships. Unique slices of the self can include
hobbies, spirituality, and education. Each slice of the self impacts the
others. For example, if there is difficulty with work, the family, finances,
and mental health will likely be impacted in a negative manner. Conversely, if an individual has employment that is fulfilling and rewarding,
this will positively impact other pieces of the self.

The universal slice of the self that has been discussed in this chapter is
finances. Finances are considered universal because they affect each individual. A well-rounded self will likely be able to demonstrate thoughtful
and managed finances. The individual struggling with finances may experience trouble with family matters, home, and emotional well-being.

Most midlife individuals will have to look closely at how they think
about money when they are faced with being sandwiched between their
children and their elders. Midlife people who have struggled financially
are especially vulnerable when aging parents need help and their children

are still in the nest. Preparation is the key factor for all midlifers as they age. Each caregiver or potential caregiver must develop a financial plan that first sustains the self and then addresses the needs of those around her. If this task appears to be too big, or insurmountable, the individual is advised to seek financial counsel. Setting aside even a small amount of money for the self each week can be a way to acknowledge that the caregiver is important. Ask for contributions from other family members in the form of finances or help around the house. As the midlife whirl gets under way, acknowledgment that the self is important and that assistance is needed to sustain the family is crucial. Find the voice that is within to speak about challenging subjects, and the long journey will be eased.

SEVEN

Creating Meaning in All Stages of Life

CASE EXAMPLE: MEANING IN ALL THINGS

Samantha grew up in a family that liked to celebrate. Birthdays and holidays were always huge events, and she can look back and clearly recall the anticipation she always felt for upcoming yearly celebrations. Her mother also created many family traditions that Samantha remembers with fondness. Each Christmas Eve everyone in the family would receive a new set of matching pajamas to wear on Christmas morning, and there would be the traditional hot chocolate in Santa mugs with their names scrolled on them. Her father would always read "The Night before Christmas" to the children from an old copy of the book that he had when he was a child. In the early years, the family would bake and decorate cookies for Santa, and each child would make one special cookie to leave under the tree. A picture would be taken of the cookies before and after Santa arrived, and the pictures would be framed in ornaments and hung on the tree with pictures from the previous years. Even when they were teenagers and when they returned home after they had launched as young adults, they liked to continue the traditions. For each family member, the rituals that had been established when the children were young created a bond and family memories that filled them with warmth and deepening love for each other. The first year that Samantha could not be home for Christmas, she missed the traditions. She found herself making a cup of hot chocolate when she woke alone on that Christmas morning.

The rituals established by Samantha's parents during the early years continued to be celebrated as the family grew through the years. These rituals were meaningful on many levels, solidifying the family members' commitment to each other and to the traditions they had formed. As the years passed, each ritual took on different meaning. When the children were young, making the "best" cookie for Santa was clearly important, manifested by the colorful sparkles, curious shapes, and an extraordinary mess. Santa's preferred cookie was always noted in the morning as the one with the biggest bite missing. As the children got older, the cookies became more elaborate in terms of taste, with the teens competing to make the most delicious batch for consuming on Christmas Day. Regardless of the goal of the year for the cookies, the underlying meaning was always that the family would create together and mark Christmas Eve with companionship and playful competition.

There were also rituals in Samantha's family that did not surround the holidays or birthdays. Some rituals occurred on a daily basis, and others were spontaneous, but each served to mark the uniqueness of Samantha's home life and strengthened their identity as a family.

Included in some of the daily rituals were consistent expectations regarding events that would occur during the daily routine. While these daily events may not seem to be important enough to call rituals, they created a structure for the family that formed its foundation. The children knew that they would be woken up at a particular time each school morning and that breakfast would be at the table with their mother. They also knew that they were expected to make their beds and make sure that their personal space was tidy. Each part of the daily routine was a small ritual that gave them information about their family and how it was expected to run. The children could make meaning from the routine; they knew that they were cared about and that they had to contribute to the family by taking care of their personal environment. When they were old enough, they had tasks that contributed to the greater good of the family and the planet—for example, by practicing sustainability by recycling and ensuring lights were out and by being kind to each other and their pets. These daily rituals combined to form each individual personality within the family in a way that also connected the family members to each other. The rituals continued throughout the day, with events such as an expected dinnertime, a homework hour, and bedtime. Clearly, the underlying meaning in Samantha's family system was that it was a consistent family with expected routine. The children could feel the safety of the routine and were not subject to tremendous chaos, worry about what might happen next, or confusion about their roles in the family. Rituals would shift and alter to meet the age-appropriate needs of the children as they grew.

In looking back at her history with her parents, Samantha does not think of her daily routine as rituals; she can, however, clearly see how the daily structure developed by her parents helped the family to define itself. The many other celebratory events from her childhood not only bring her happy memories but also serve to create a foundation for celebrations and meaning-making in her own family. Samantha hopes her own children will someday want to implement some of the traditions that came from her upbringing and initially from their grandparents before them. Generations of meaning-making could be created as Samantha's family traditions and rituals are passed down. Samantha likes the idea of keeping pieces of her extended family history intact throughout the years, and she consciously maintains much of her parents' structure and many of their celebrations.

MEANING IN ALL SHAPES AND SIZES

Merriam-Webster's Collegiate Dictionary defines *meaning* as "something meant or intended" and as a "significant quality . . . implication of a hidden or special significance."[1]

The meaning of life that is created within an individual and a family can truly come in all shapes, designs, colors, and sizes. Meaning that develops within an individual or environmental context can have many dimensions, such as being small and inconsequential, all encompassing, directive, or instructive. The meaning that is created can cause happiness, joy, anger, fear, or harm.

Meaning regarding the self and the world is created at a very early stage in human development and progresses as the infant grows in concert with the environment around him.[2] This developing meaning will create part of the frame for the individual's personality, which in turn will impact his family and the greater world around him.

MEANING THAT IS CREATED BY STRUCTURE AND LOVE

It is much easier to build a life that is rich with positive meaning and the desire to do good things if one is raised in an environment that promotes this concept. Good enough parenting provides a foundation within which the individual can grow and have a healthy concept of the self.[3] This good enough parenting generally includes a structure in which the family develops a routine that helps each member to know what is expected. The parents in this family provide warm praise and appropriate consequences for behaviors. The family's routines are small rituals that occur daily, and the transmission of kindness and warmth helps each family member to build rituals based on love. In the family that functions with thoughtful affection, this sense of goodness is transmitted to the children and to the world around them. The meaning in this family, while it may not even be consciously thought about, is a positive life force. The rituals in the family that naturally arise from such a positive environment are filled with love, joy, and affection. The development of meaning within individuals in the family also creates a sense of purpose and action. For each individual, purpose gives force to the journey and to the development of what she loves most. Meaning can build as the design and fulfillment of one's purpose expand throughout the course of one's life. In the structured, safe routine of the affectionate family, meaning and purpose become interwoven, and the values of the self are formed. Positive energy surrounds the journey into adulthood and the continued transmission of loving routines, rituals, and happiness.

Finding the path and meaning in life may simply mean becoming more conscious of one's choices. There are simple questions that individuals can ask themselves to begin to tease out their purpose in living. Each individual has a unique trajectory that will be unlike any other person's path. In reflecting on the questions that will be posed in this chapter, you may find that you have been living your life with greater purpose than you have imagined.

Reflection Exercise

The Big Question that most people have asked themselves at varying times in their life is "What is the purpose of life?" There may be moments when it seems that existence is just a series of days that have no meaning. In a busy life, there is often little time or opportunity to sit and ponder meaning. Without consideration, as the days blend into one another with the same tasks, these questions will likely arise on their own: "Why am I doing this?" "Why am I here?"

The following questions may be helpful in reminding you of your purpose and why perhaps you may be living this unique life of yours.

Settle into a quiet spot and ask these questions. Be a gentle investigator of your own thoughts and feelings, and take a moment to jot down what comes to mind. There are no right or wrong answers; just allow your mind to flow, and information will take you, as the investigator, down the path to meaning. You may choose to answer the questions in a different order from which they are listed. The questions can be asked and then put aside to ponder on another day. This exercise is meant to help you begin to think more consciously about how you live your life and how your actions create meaning. Embrace the questions, and enjoy the thoughts they bring up for you. If you like, answer the questions with a partner, friend, or loved one.

1. What are my passions in life?
2. How do I act on these passions? Do I make time in my day to express them? If not, how can I schedule times for them?
3. Am I happy with how I am living my life? Why or why not?
4. What can I do to become happier each day?
5. What is "everyday" greatness? How can I instill some of my unique greatness into each day?[4]
6. What do others tell me I am really good at?
7. What is the greatest opportunity I have missed in life? Is there anything I can do to replicate this opportunity in some other fashion to repair the loss?
8. If I had seven days to live, how would I spend them?

As you delve into each question, a multitude of thoughts that create greater self-understanding can emerge. For example, as you address Question 5 (What is "everyday" greatness?), you may come to a clearer understanding that each day you attempt to be as kind as possible. This revelation may solidify the knowledge that this is a key component of your personality, and you can take purpose and meaning from this revelation. The Big Question of "Why?" regarding the purpose of one's life, can slowly come to be answered through the process of self-discovery. Question 5 may lead you to become more aware that your kindnesses have helped others, and this simple understanding may provide you with reasons for your existence. The thoughts and reasons that answer the question "Why am I here?" do not have to be earth-shattering. You do not have to have saved the planet from destruction or to have created a masterpiece. Seemingly small and inconsequential acts can create far-reaching positive consequences; it can sometimes take reflecting on one's life to make these acts conscious and to realize that they are, in fact, important and that they create purpose in living.

Another example of how these questions may help you to make meaning of your life can be found in Question 1 (What are my passions?) and

Question 2 (How do I act on my passions?). As you examine your passions, you may become more aware that you love dancing or baseball. The love of this activity or sport brings you joy and organizes your free time. Families can share the love of the activity or sport, or certain family members may bond around it. Great meaning through the generations can be made as the passion is shared. Generations in a family can pass down a love of baseball, for example, and bond around this shared passion. They may gather around the television to watch their favorite team, share this activity with an elder who is a fan of the sport, attend a special yearly game, and teach young children in the family the sport.

A favored question of this author is Question 8 (If I had seven days to live, how would I spend them?). Would the way we choose to spend our time in life be different if we were aware of just how time-limited our existence could be? This question encourages you to identify the important people, places, and perhaps unresolved areas in your life that require attention. It may cause you to examine the things that you have missed in life and the things that you have not said to those who are important to you. Reflection on this question may give you the opportunity, as desired, to rectify these situations. When we go through life thinking that we have forever to deal with old issues or to go places or try new foods, these events can be held off for another day. Once the realization occurs that, indeed, our time on this planet is limited and that it may end in an instant, it becomes clearer that some things are more important than others. If you knew with certainty that you had only seven days to live, would you continue to get up and go to work? How important is that to you? Or would it be important to design your last week in other ways, such as spending time with family and friends? Would you choose to, finally, fly for a few days to the Caribbean island you have always dreamed of visiting? Or attend the Metropolitan Opera? Or hop a freight train? What might be important to one person may not seem important to another, as individuals have different hopes and dreams for their lives. By asking yourself Question 8, you will become acutely aware of what is most important to you and where your meaning and passion in the world lie.

The unfortunate reality in this life is that none of us really know when we will die. Death could happen in a matter of seconds to one who had expected a great deal of time to complete unfinished business. Or one may live to a ripe old age and have the luxury of living out his every wish. People who live each moment as if it may be their last will likely have many fewer regrets as they lay dying. These people will have found their passion and meaning in the world and will have used their lives to fulfill their purpose. Fulfillment and meaning will come in many sizes and packages that will be defined by the individual. There are no rights or wrongs, only regrets if chances are missed or ignored.

Question 8 can be adapted in many ways. For example, the question could be asked reducing the seven-day time frame to one day, or it could be asked increasing the time frame to a month, or even a year. The responses may initially look different; however, it is likely that in between the lines will fall what is most relevant and important to the core of the person answering the question. Some responses may be laced with the need for fulfilling relationships and spending the last quality moments with loved ones. Others may have projects that are especially important to complete, their own legacies to be left behind. Yet others may have places to which they wish to travel. The core of the individual's personality will shape how she makes her meaning in life and may also clarify it in the thoughts of upcoming death.

You can revisit this reflection exercise and the questions listed above throughout the course of your life. You may find that your answers shift and change as you experience different developmental stages and as circumstances alter. There will likely be times in your life when the Big Question of "Why?" seems to be scrolled everywhere; creating a more conscious life can provide answers that may help you to move forward with purpose and renewed passion.

MEANING THAT IS CREATED BY CHAOS AND TRAUMA

The opposite of structure and love can be seen as chaos and trauma. Unfortunately, as easily as positive meaning can be created within a healthy environment, negative meaning can also be created with ease in an existence that is surrounded by disruption and evil.

The young person who is raised in a family in which there is substance abuse, inconsistency, and abuse is likely to come to believe that the world is cruel and unsafe. Some early home environments are toxic and infuse the growing youngster with hurtful sights, sounds, and sensations that can leave a lasting impact. The unhealthy home can contribute to the development of a core personality that is filled with rage, sadness, and a desire for revenge or withdrawal. Some children who are raised in environments of chaos and evil, or some variation of these elements, may have enough resilience to rise above the negative impact and thrive. Others do not have this strength; therefore, they take on some of the characteristics and beliefs of the environment in which they were raised. The meaning that these youngsters develop can have a negative purpose, and their passion may be to hurt the world right back.

Chaos alone is not necessarily enough to drive a person into the development of a negative self-core and negative meaning-making. Some homes that are chaotic are also loving and warm. Growing up in a chaotic, yet loving family can lead an individual to develop a healthy set of values. However, if the chaos is combined with derision and ill will, it is more likely that the growing person will pick up the nuances of destructiveness that surround him and perpetuate them into the world as an adult. This person is likely to develop conduct or personality disorders and inflict pain in his relationships. He has been so badly wounded that the meaning at the root of both his unconscious impulse and his conscious action is distorted with anger and pain. Many of these people end up in the criminal justice system; they are batterers and abusers, and they design their lives with the purpose of creating upheaval.

As stated, the meaning and purpose of an individual's life can come in many shapes and sizes and are first influenced in the early years of her development. If one is lucky enough to be born into a home that is structured and loving, it is likely that one will develop a passion for good things. For those who draw the short straw and are raised in an environment that is chaotic and filled with trauma, it is more likely that the life purpose and meaning they develop will be heavily influenced by disorder and conflict.

There is good news for individuals who have developed a negative path in their lives. One of the great gifts we have been provided in this life is that as humans we can choose to change. For a growing youngster in a violent and chaotic home, the best way to stay safe from harm is to blend into the environment. However, as that child grows into adulthood, he has choices that he can make to find better adaptation and healthier meaning in his life. A good example of how an individual who has lived in an environment of evil can change his core meaning can be seen in our prisons. Those who become prisoners suddenly, perhaps for the first time in their lives, have a consistent and structured environment in which they know what to expect at any given time of the day. Prisoners also have a great deal of time on their hands to assess their lives and look at the purpose and meaning in their existence. Many of them are drawn to religion and, ultimately, to forgiveness. While it is true that some prison converts are conning the system, their families, and perhaps themselves, some are genuine in their wish to change. They have made a conscious decision to use the rest of their lives, in jail or not, to promote good. This is a dramatic shift in meaning and purpose. If these individuals are released, it remains to be seen if the shift from chaos to structure and good can survive. Some may revert back to the old, familiar ways in which they were raised. For a few, however, their life purpose can change for the better.

The examples of meaning-making and purpose have been dramatic in this chapter to illustrate how purpose can develop from an early age. The reality is that most of us will likely find ourselves developing passions in our lives that are not such polar opposites (good versus evil) and so distinct. For example, most of us will have some of the positive purpose that makes us want to become better parents, partners, and citizens. Laced with that good purpose may be moments of behaving poorly, acting out, and creating a sort of chaos in our own generally stable environments. This is the fate of being human. We may strive to achieve our best selves but fall short of the mark at times. Likewise, the person whose core meaning is centered on revenge and destruction may still have a deep love for her children and develop some relationships in which she strives to be selfless.

MAKING MULTIGENERATIONAL MEANING

Caregivers who are reading this chapter may wonder what kind of meaning they are transmitting to those around them. It is an excellent question, and it is hoped that you will finding an answer from reading this book. Meaning within a family can be made in all kinds of ways. It can be overt, with designed rituals and family functions that bind the family together. Or meaning may be made in more covert, nondirective ways, such as the daily structure of the family and the expectations that are created by routine.

Family culture, interests, and unique celebrations create meaning for the youngsters, midlife caregivers, and elders in the family. In previous generations in American culture, the family was composed primarily of a nuclear group that included the parents and the children. In this century, that pattern is changing, and our culture is adopting the ways of other societies that have long included the multigenerational family group. In the South Pacific islands of Micronesia, families of up to 30 members may live in the same home and share the same food. The workers bring home their money and share it with the family to buy the necessities needed to survive. Elders are well respected and provided with the best of the food, shelter, and comforts. Children may be "adopted" informally within the village. If there is not enough food or shelter in one extended family, the next villager will take in one or two of the children until times improve. There is no legal system for this sharing of care; it is a tradition that continues because it works well. Children feel loved by many; they understand who their biological parents are and also that they have many aunties and others who take care of them. The boundaries of the family system are permeable, and the children feel they belong in each village family compound. Because the villagers survive using a shared model of sustainment, they take care of one another.

In this way, the multigenerational family takes on an even greater extension in some countries. Imagine if this system of shared shelter, food, and love were to occur in our neighborhoods. It is ironic that in third-world countries some of the best family care is given to all members of the system, but sometimes this care is not provided in our own well-developed nation. In many third-world countries, there are no nursing homes; each village family cares for its own until death. The clear meaning in these villages is that all people will be loved, cherished, and cared for until they part from this world. Recently, in one of these village families, the patriarch passed away. He was a virile elder of 78, a deacon in the village church, and the leader of a large extended family of 35 family members. He died suddenly in the middle of the night of a heart attack while walking to the outhouse and was found by one of the children in the morning. The entire island mourned the loss of this amazing man who would take in children and other villagers when they needed shelter. His extended family consisted of hundreds of islanders and even visitors from other countries. His eldest son became the new patriarch of the family, while the mourning went on for weeks in celebrations and rituals that took many cultural forms. Western influence was in evidence in the form of T-shirts made by the family that read "Goodbye Pahpa Sakies, Have a Good Trip."

The Micronesian system of caregiving is likely found in many other countries that struggle with poverty, disease, and famine. It is interesting to note that, as our culture moves ahead, we follow the lead of less-privileged nations in caring for more than one generation of family. There are many important lessons about love and purpose that can be learned from the examples of other cultures. The nuclear family system no longer works for our generation; we have moved into a phase in which we see more clearly that we need to take care of each other.

As human beings, we experience one powerful common phenomenon from birth to death: the need to be loved. While some may say that this is not important to them, it is likely that on some level they want to be cherished by others in some way. The powers of love and caring, which create structure and purpose, all help individuals to design their reasons for existence. The Big Question of "Why?" may have the simplest of answers: we exist to love and be loved.

RITUALS, REMEMBERING, AND CELEBRATIONS

There are many ways to create meaning, as has been explored in this chapter. This section will list some specific rituals, ways to remember, and celebrations that can create meaning. This list is in no way comprehensive; your own family will have many unique ways of making meaning that create substance for your family's identity. The rituals that are offered in this section can be added to any family's current repertoire to fortify connection and meaning within the family.

The ritual is a symbolic way in which any individual or community (religious group, social group, family, etc.) designs a form of communication that expresses the values of that person or group. Rituals may be celebratory; they may also reflect remembrances of things past or repeated traditions. The ritual is one way in which the individual and the community can make meaning of life events. As discussed in this chapter, some of the rituals that create meaning may appear to be negative or even evil. Many rituals, however, are celebrations.

Examples of Rituals That Occur throughout the Generations

- Religious rituals: church services, first communion, circumcision, bar and bat mitzvahs, baptism, marriage, divorce, holiday worship, rites of passage, sacrifice, funerals, satanic ceremonies;
- Legal rituals: marriage, divorce, purchasing a home, going to court, oaths of allegiance, politics, involvement with law enforcement;
- Family rituals: birth of a child, death of a family member, celebrations of birthdays, coming-of-age celebrations, graduations, wakes, anniversaries, special food/drink, health care routines, family games;
- Social rituals: clubs, hobbies, sports, parades, handshaking, music, dancing, parties, fraternities/sororities, volunteering; and
- Other rituals: work events, daily routines, popular television shows, using special utensils; purchasing a car/boat; attending college.

At first glance, these rituals may seem like everyday events that most individuals experience at some point in their lifetime. On closer examination, each of the listed events can be identified as a situation that holds meaning and can be an organizing factor for how individuals in the family relate to one another. For example, church services may be a central way the generations in a family make sense of their existence and their relationships to each other. The children in this family may be raised to believe the same religious concepts that the elders hold close, and the entire family may attend the same church for generations.

Watching television is yet another daily activity that may be a ritual. For example, there might be a special show that the entire family gathers to watch each evening. In some families, television time may be scheduled after dinner with an elder as a way to provide companionship. Elders come to understand that this television time is reserved especially for them, and they likely take away the impression that they are cared about. Even if an elder is demented and may not be able to understand conversation, the time devoted to watching television or other interactions provides the sensation that he is important enough to have special time and attention.

The rituals that individuals, families, and communities create are ways to celebrate, remember, and build connection and love. Meaning will naturally arise from the creation of rituals and a thoughtful life. This meaning will help to provide individuals with the comfort of knowing that they have a purpose in this life and assist them in answering the Big Question of "Why?"

EIGHT

Conclusion

Strength for the Sandwich Generation has provided a general description of the phenomenon of midlife and the impact of caring for both one's children and one's elders during this developmental middle-life stage. The introduction to this book described how midlife challenges alone can be sufficient to create stress and adversity for an individual. Yet, in this generation, many midlife people are also managing the care of their growing children and their aging parents as they attempt to navigate their own life hurdles. This book has provided a guide to those traveling the midlife path while providing multigenerational care to their family members. This journey can be one that is overwhelming at times. Embedded in this work have been suggestions for managing the flow of responsibilities, caring for oneself, and finding joy in a modified and healthier role as a multigenerational caregiver.

The second chapter of the book identified some of the biological, cultural, financial, and social factors that individuals are faced with at midlife. Also explored was the well-known midlife crisis event or period, during which the individual evaluates her past and what she wants for the future. The impact of a midlife event on personality and future development was assessed, and solutions were offered to assist in making this a productive time in the life span. Psychological and physical factors of the middle years were detailed, and issues that can arise during this period were illuminated. The chapter described many of the characteristics of the individual who, at midlife, can find herself sandwiched between her children and her parents. Solutions were also offered to make the middle years more productive, happier, and enriched by opportunities to grow.

The next chapter provided information regarding the joys and trials of parenting during midlife. While parenting presents many challenges, there are also many moments of delight and extraordinary beauty. Slowing down and taking stock of the good times and all the positive events that take place were emphasized. Emotional, financial, and philosophical issues related to the raising of children while attending to aging parents were examined, and creative ways of managing the load were offered. The concept of providing structure within the family system was described as key to maintaining a healthy self and family. In this way, each member of the system knows what to expect and when to expect it; chaos is diminished as the main caregivers establish routines around which the family revolves.

Caring for one's elders in the context of the multigenerational family system was next explored. Elderly parents become more vulnerable as they age and need more assistance to function effectively and healthfully. In the fourth chapter, some of the complications of caring for one's elders that can arise out of the early relationship between the elder and the midlife adult were reviewed. If the early relationship between them was loving and positive, it is likely that this love will be reflected in the way the midlife adult cares for his aging parent. Likewise, if the earlier relationship was based on negative interactions, the midlife caregiver may experience ambivalence in taking care of his parents. The bond between any parent and child can be positive or negative; if a relationship has been negative, this may be corrected during the later years if there is the desire to do so. Suggestions for improving the individual's bonds with his elderly parents were offered within the fourth chapter. The concept of forgiveness was addressed, along with a description of how the act of forgiving can be helpful to both the person who is being forgiven and the person who is forgiving. Additionally, this chapter addresses the emotional aspects of impending loss as the adult child watches his parents age. The feelings associated with losing one's parents can be overwhelmingly sad for some individuals, can be a relief to others, and for others can create a sense of unfinished business. The upcoming death of loved ones may also stimulate new thoughts regarding the finality of life and crystallize some typical midlife questions regarding why each of us is placed on this planet. This chapter explored these questions and the midlifer's role while balancing the care of children and parents. The elderly parent can require both emotional and physical care, and tips were provided for meeting both these types of needs. The chapter concluded with suggestions for creating joint meaning among the children in the family, the midlife caregiver, and the elder as the days of life together dwindle.

The concept of the self was strengthened and fortified in the fifth chapter. This portion of the book provided a reminder of the basic needs of the self, especially for those who are in a position of multigenerational caregiving. As a caregiver, the individual may often feel that she is being pulled in opposite directions and that she can never do all there is to accomplish. There may not appear to be enough time in the day to do all that needs to be done. This chapter included the Caregiver's Creed, which articulates the premise that, unless care of the self comes first, no family members will truly have their needs met. The fifth chapter emphasized the importance of making time for the self and one's partner and of asking for help from others. Caregivers, by nature, often put themselves last and then feel resentful when they do not have time for themselves or when they feel overwhelmed by the tasks they have to complete. This chapter encouraged caregivers to put their own needs at the top of the list through the Caregiver's Creed. The nuts and bolts of creating a plan to manage each piece of multigenerational caregiving were described to assist those in the Sandwich Generation. Individuals can adapt the sample plan laid out in this chapter so that it fits their own lifestyles and includes caretaking time for everyone, beginning with themselves.

Managing money is a most challenging aspect of life even under the best of circumstances. In the traditional nuclear family with two parents and two children, money issues can often impact such things as the schools that the children attend, the food that the family eats, the vacations that the family takes, and the new clothing that the family purchases. In the current financial climate, many families are reevaluating just how they spend their salaries and considering how to stretch each dollar. As the nuclear family evolves into a multigenerational family structure, money is stretched even thinner. Not only do the parents want to save for their retirement, but also they are planning for college for the kids and often paying for the care of the elders in the family. Financial stress is huge, creating emotional upheaval. The sixth chapter addressed ways for the family to manage theses financial challenges. Creating a mindful, open approach to discussing, allocating, and distributing money was explored in this chapter. This chapter contained resources for the financial journey of the multigenerational caregiver.

As the individual enters midlife with a complex set of variables to navigate, he may find himself asking age-old questions, especially questions regarding his purpose in life and the meaning to be found in it, which can emerge at full force during midlife. The person entering his middle years will likely be dealing with questions about his past, where he has come from, and where he wants to go during the next phase of his life.

He will also likely have children he is preparing to launch into the world, and perhaps he will have elderly parents, as well, who are facing their final years. The multigenerational caregiver may feel overwhelmed by the many tasks he performs and by the complex emotions that occur during the different developmental stages of his children and elders. Creating meaning from the previous generations of family functioning may be one way in which the midlife individual can develop reasons to move ahead and find answers to his own internal questions. The midlife person is steering the family ship, and if he can find a course that helps the entire family to bond together more fully and create shared meaning, the voyage will be less rocky. The seventh chapter offered the reader suggestions for the creation of small rituals and patterns that assist the family system in blending together more seamlessly through the shared development of meaning. These rituals and patterns can be newly designed or come from the practices of previous generations. As they are implemented and practiced, the multigenerational family develops its own traditions that can live forward in time for generations to come. A practiced use of traditions can be powerful and can assist individuals in the family in finding their answers to questions regarding their purpose in life. The use of rituals, celebrations, and remembrances was detailed to assist the caregiver in addressing the existential components of each life stage and building on interactions with each family member during the different developmental stages.

At the book's close, the author describes her life as a multigenerational family caregiver and shares some of her own trials and successes. Appendix A provides a list of resources for the multigenerational caregiver, and Appendix B repeats the Caregiver's Creed.

The goal of this work has been to encourage, support, and provide meaning for those who are doing multiple tasks at multiple times each day in an effort to care for their loved ones. The most important role of the multigenerational caregiver is the transmission of love to loved ones; all else is secondary. The task is to try to remember this most important role as the day's activities assault the senses. Stop, breathe, and carry forth with tenderness toward oneself and others. There is no more important job.

AFTERWORD

The Author's Story

There have been moments during the writing of this book that have been cathartic, painful, joyful, and tremendously challenging. I began this writing with the idea that it would be an easy book to write because I am a member of the Sandwich Generation and, therefore, am experiencing all the dynamics that I had intended to write about. I found that my experience was quite the opposite and that my writing did not flow with ease. There were months that I could not write a word because I was so caught up in the emotions of the time or overwhelmed by my life and all the other tasks that I needed to accomplish. By far, the emotional part of journey has been the most challenging for me, and putting into words what I have wanted to convey to help the reader has been quite hard. I have had to work hard to separate my personal experience from the words of the book in order to present an organized, linear discussion. My own process of living with children and elderly parents has influenced this writing and inspired the book, while also clouding the writing with my own great sorrows, trials, and joys.

I am a 55-year-old woman with a touch of gray beginning at my temples. Although I am a survivor of divorce, late-stage cancer, and other life challenges, the last two years have been the hardest of my life, a time when my sorrow has seemed to have no bounds. There have been moments when I have been stopped in my footsteps from the emotional pain and had tears rolling down my cheeks as I sobbed my grief. The car has been my solace; in driving back and forth to work, I have the quiet space of a half-hour to myself, and I let the tears find their release. The unimaginable emotional pain comes and goes. I try to let it come when it needs release and stay with it, to live in the moment as much as I can, and to honor my sadness.

I am blessed and one of those lucky midlife women who also experiences moments of unfettered joy. The moments of joy contrast with the pain and at times create this schizophrenic-like existence, but I roll with it. I suppose there are other options, like plodding along in the comfort of unconsciousness or denial, but that does not suit me.

I let myself cry, I let myself be silly and playful, and I love as hard as I can. These things I have learned from my mother, and I embrace them. My favorite picture of my mother sits on my desk at work. It is a black-and-white photograph, and she is smoking a cigarette, lounging back on a couch wearing leopard tights, and looking seductive and playful. My mother gave me my spirit, the love I have for all living things and for adventure. She pushed me to travel and to study and to embrace all the facets of life. One of her favorite quotes was "You have to try everything at least once." My mother is now 78 years old, and she and my father live with us in a small complex we built that connects our two conservative homes with an inside hallway. She is in remarkably good physical health; her body's wellness contrasts dramatically with her state of mind. My mother has late-stage dementia; sometimes she knows who I am, and sometimes she asks me who I am or if I am her mother. Her Alzheimer's disease has progressed significantly in the last three years, and I now have to bathe her and cut her meat.

I have four stepdaughters who are gifts to the world. The oldest two have launched and are making their way in different parts of the country. The eldest is in the arts and the other in business. The younger children are ages 10 and 11 at this writing, and my husband and I have joint custody of them. They live with our family for half of each week, but we participate in their activities without boundaries. I work full-time at the local university and supervise a staff of 30 health care workers and mental health providers; it is an awesome job and rewarding. My husband, bless his heart, at age 62 has recently cut back at work to half-time. In my spare time, I am a writer, a Red Cross volunteer, and an avid reader.

Many of my life's responsibilities came as choice. I chose to become a psychologist, I chose my place of employment, and I chose to marry a man with four daughters. I also choose to volunteer and to write. As I age, my life choices become more difficult to manage, as I tire more easily. The many balls I juggle now sometimes fall to the ground because I find I cannot keep them all in the air at the same time.

The aspects of my life that I would not have chosen are those that surround my parents. My choice would have been for them to be healthy and to be able to spend their remaining years in comfort and ease. My father has fallen several times and has a steel bar that creates the link from his hip to his leg. He has a thin frame and is wobbly, and while his mind is as sharp as a tack, his body is failing. My mother requires constant attention and cueing with all her daily functions. I am blessed that they live with us; I only wish that they could better enjoy this time in their lives.

It is challenging to put myself first. I have to work at it. My husband and I have had to plan our lives so that everything is handy and we can be at home as much as possible for both the children and the elders. My morning begins at 5:00 A.M., when I exercise for 30 minutes on the treadmill in our garage. I consider this time for myself, and I can plan my day as I walk. I am still multitasking as I exercise by entertaining my three cats with the motion of the treadmill, and they dart back and forth as they play around me. My pets love the morning and scratch at the garage door to get out to begin our exercise routine. After we exercise, the shower is another place that rejuvenates me before I meet the full force of the day. There are times that as I exercise, I cry, or I unleash my sadness in the shower that follows. I am mostly weeping for my mother: how much I miss her, how lucky I am to still have her, how sad I am when she has the moments of realization that she has Alzheimer's disease.

My wonderful husband gets the kids out of bed after I have left the house, makes their breakfast, and gets them on the bus. I am so sorry that I must miss these morning rituals; I always leave the three of them a love note and call them while they are eating from my desk at the office. I cherish the few mornings that I have a holiday or snow day and can have breakfast with my family.

My father takes charge of Mom in the mornings, helping her dress and making her breakfast. She has the same grilled sandwich each morning with her cranberry-grape juice and coffee, and each morning she tells Dad it is the most delicious sandwich she has ever eaten. My father has developed a pattern for their day. After breakfast, Mom naps, and he sits in his chair and snoozes. He then takes her for a ride; sometimes they have lunch at McDonald's or another place with easy access for him. Some days, when the weather permits, they sit out on the lawn in their chairs and feel the sun on their faces. Mom will often cry for no known reason and cannot generally articulate what makes her sad. There are times she is briefly aware of her dementia, and she cries about this, and she sometimes says she is sad because she misses her mother. She is sweet, and it is painful to witness her loss again and again.

After lunch, they both nap, although Mom has taken to wandering, a development that makes it difficult for Dad to rest. If my mother is not constantly monitored, she will get into mischief like a two-year-old. For example, one day we noticed Mom was not wearing her wedding rings, which we found weeks later hidden in a sock in the bottom drawer of her bathroom. She can become stubborn and refuse to take her pills or to put on her underwear. When we are able to tag-team her care, it works best; she will generally respond to one of us. At age 82, Dad has the patience of a saint. I marvel at my father and how gentle he is with Mom. He explains everything to her even though she does not grasp a word of what he is saying. At this stage in her illness, she cannot understand words and says, "What?" after anything that is spoken to her. It is not her hearing; her brain cannot process language anymore. She can no longer write, even her name. My mother loved to read, and now she cannot comprehend language, either spoken or written. She sits with clothing advertisement booklets and goes through them all day, folding down pictures of the outfits she likes.

My workday is busy, and the hours fly by. Unless there is an emergency at home or at school with the kids, the day at the office passes in a predictable manner. In remembering to take my own medicine, I practice self-care by making sure I take time for lunch and pace my day; I also take a nap on the couch in my office as the day permits. My staff members are all also fond of my couch, as they know they are welcome to take refresher naps when it is available. The crises and small fires I put out daily at work seem small in comparison to my home events; I must believe this is because I can look at the work issues with more objectivity. My job is almost a respite, the place where I can breathe between work situations and appointments. While I still have some clamoring from staff for my attention, it is manageable, and I can shut my door.

At home, I can seldom completely close the door. While I can request space and set boundaries, I am the one who is always "on." Even after everyone has gone to bed if someone is ill or when the smoke alarm goes off, I am the person "in charge" to right the wrong.

The drive home from work at the end of the day requires several conscious tasks. The first is to shut the door on what has occurred in the office that day; this is a task I continually have to work on, as I am in constant contact with my job through my Blackberry and email. There are some evenings I am more successful with shutting down work than others. I have found that I can be more present at home if I allow myself to check my email periodically during the evening to assure myself that no new work crises have occurred. The second task for the drive home is to center myself and prepare for the circus that awaits me as I enter my home.

I breathe deeply and listen to music; sometimes I call a friend and just chat, grouse, and commiserate. The car is my favorite spot. I have it all to myself, and I keep bottles of my favorite sparkling water at hand to sip as I drive. Interestingly, I also keep a change of clothing in my trunk and money stashed in my glove compartment. I think I like the idea that one day I could just keep driving into the sunset. I have an awesome function on my steering wheel that allows me to change channels on the radio with a flip of my finger. On my drive home, I can return personal telephone calls and make contact with the outside world separate from my job and family. The best part is that I am not interrupted. It is my ride, my time.

I pull into the garage and take a deep breath, collect my briefcase and miscellaneous work paraphernalia, and open the door. The cats have heard my garage door open, and they all greet me by rubbing around my legs and trying to trip me up as I carry my laptop and work paraphernalia into the house. If Mom has heard the car, she will be with the cats at the door, asking me where I have been. She always tells me she has not seen me for several days with a disapproving look. Sometimes she is crying. I attempt to make my way through the obstacle course and put my things down before they fall out of my arms. I again wonder why I carry so much baggage. Do I really need to reuse the lunch bag or coffee cup? Sustainability is going to kill me, I think.

On the nights I am really blessed, I will have the five minutes it takes me to change into comfortable clothes before the side door opens and the kids tumble through. They are wired from their day, glad to be home, and eager to tell me about their travails. Lunch boxes get thrown in my general direction, and they troupe upstairs to settle in before dinner. One child generally talks nonstop, while the other waits for her brief opening and then begins an entirely different story. Mom is lingering at the fringes of the activity, always standing right in the middle of the room, so one has to be careful not to knock her over. My husband lumbers in behind the kids; I think he hides in the garage for a while before he enters, the smart man. The flurry of lunch boxes, backpacks, and chatter continues as my husband tries to work in a kiss around the edges of the chaos. He does not get to change into comfy clothes, but his trade-off is watching the news after dinner for 30 minutes. We both move in a dance in our tiny kitchen to get dinner for six cooked and on the table. Mom generally decides she wants to help and stands in the way; I have learned that, if I give her even a simple task, it delays dinner for 20 minutes, so we ask one of the kids to take her into the next room. She can see us working from there, as we have cut a window between the kitchen and living room, and we put the television on for her to watch. At some point between the kids coming in the door and dinner being put on the table, one of us throws a load of laundry in the washer.

Dinner can go almost any way. Most nights it is an enjoyable event. Dad hobbles over from his side of the house, and Mom sits at her regular spot, although she is always surprised by it. The kids censor little, so I know we are a healthy family. They need to be reminded to use their indoor voices, not to burp out loud, and not to put a mound of butter on their potatoes. We have a two-bite rule, which means they must eat at least two spoonfuls of everything on their plate. In this way, I am assured they are at least trying new things and getting a sampling of vegetables. One of our girls loves green beans and most healthy foods; the other is our carbohydrate addict and would eat only noodles if we allowed it. They are loud and full of stories at dinner. The child who is the natural-born talker can tell the most deadly endless stories about Pokémon and other tween phenomena that are fairly meaningless to the adults. The other child continues to try to find her space in the flow of words when there is a second of silence. My husband and father generally have their own side conversation, while my mother pushes her food around and has to be reminded to eat. I have cut up her food for her, and with cueing, she manages to eat half her meal each night.

The most dangerous part of evening occurs at the end of dinner when the children have already cleared their places and been excused. I remind my mother to take her pills. My father and husband hold their breath. On the good nights, she will swallow them without much trouble. On the bad nights, she asks, for the hundredth time, why she has to take pills and what they are for, reports she doesn't need them, and tries to hide them. I must admit that *this* is the thing that makes me crazy. I become as demented as she is when it comes to those pills. It is like I am waiting for her to become obstinate so I can become a crazy person without any sense or patience. I get mad. I tell her she has to take her pills. She gets more stubborn and holds them in her fist in a tight ball. My face gets redder and redder. My father is shrinking, if possible. My husband, bless him again, intervenes.

I do not know why I reenact this silly situation with the pills almost every night. I know it is coming; like a train down the same track, it comes almost every evening. It is my fault; I am not the one with dementia; I should be sane. I recall the adage that "To do the same thing over and over again when it doesn't work is a sign of insanity." Yet each night I fall into the pill fight. I am determined she will take those pills. I lose all compassion for the woman I love so much and become Godzilla of the Pill. I cannot be rational.

And yes, of course, she always eventually takes her pills. I just don't have the 20 minutes it takes to coax and cajole her, so my husband takes over. By that time, everyone at the table is upset but Mom because she has forgotten.

If it is a night that there is an evening sporting event or school activity for the kids, we rush around like maniacs, trying to get out the door to be on time. I cannot even begin to try to describe what this looks like; just imagine it. These nights Dad does not get a break from Mom, and I feel guilty.

On the evenings there are not outside events, we fall into a routine after dinner. Dad wobbles back to his side of the house, and I take Mom over while my husband loads the dishwasher. The girls have begun their home-work, or I have started a bath for them.

Dad finally has his free time after dinner when I take over Mom's care for a few hours. I try to keep this time sacred for him because he has had a full day of my mother, and, frankly, I have trouble with just the few hours I watch over her. Dad sits with his crossword puzzles for an hour and then plays solitaire on his computer until I bring Mom home before bed.

Mom is, for the most part, very sweet. On their side of the house, I pre-pare my parents' bed and put the powder under the sheets that Dad likes. I cue Mom to undress, repeating each article of clothing that must come off, often several times. She will look up at me with big eyes and ask again, "Take off my shirt?" It breaks my heart. Just two years ago Mom was able to manage her own basic care needs. The Alzheimer's disease has pro-gressed quickly and without mercy. It is a hateful illness. Both Mom and I are survivors of breast cancer. But even with Mom's mastectomy and my chemo, radiation, multiple surgeries, and the many side effects that have pursued me through the years, the cancer holds no candle to the horror of Alzheimer's disease.

After we get Mom in her nightie, we proceed to the bathroom to take out her teeth, brush them, wash her face, and apply cream. Once a week I bathe her completely and wash her hair. This is a somewhat traumatic event for my mom, as she is afraid of the water, but we manage somehow, with me getting a shower in the bargain. I praise her continually through her grooming. There are times she asks me who I am. There are times she cries for her mother. I constantly have to shake off my own moments of sadness.

After grooming, I bring her back to our side of the house and settle her in the television room to watch half-hour sitcoms. She likes Kramer on Jerry Seinfeld's show and laughs out loud when he bumps into things.

I am always grateful when she recognizes someone on television or laughs at something she finds funny. She often asks me what the characters just said, and I know this is because she cannot digest the language.

In the meantime, my heroic husband has cleaned up the kitchen and is watching his 30 minutes of news, has fallen asleep on the couch, or is helping one of our daughters with her math homework. I will have thrown the laundry into the dryer by now and may even be folding clothes while I sit with Mom. She likes to help fold and actually does a good job with this task, perhaps remembering how to fold from some corner of her long-term memory. I like to include her in this task because it helps her to feel accomplished.

The kids and cats come in and out of the television room, the kids sometimes briefly watching the show with us. They prefer their own tween entertainment channels, and generally they don't stay for long. Some nights we have a situation that requires a family meeting, and Mom sits with us as we talk. Other nights I sneak out of the television room to make the kids' snacks; they currently like nachos broiled and smothered in cheese or Italian ice or fruit. While I am making snacks, I am also making school lunches and setting the table for the next evening. If I am lucky, Mom stays in the television room while I am in and out accomplishing these tasks. Hubby has certainly fallen asleep in front of the other TV by now, and I am happy he is resting. I peek at my laptop continually throughout the evening to see what has arrived in my inbox from work and if it needs attention.

I take Mom back to Dad at 8:30. He and Mom watch some more television for an hour and then retire to bed. Mom drinks her one and one-half glasses of cream sherry, which she never forgets. Dad will have a stiff scotch. Who can blame him?

Back with my little family, I scurry upstairs to spend time with the girls. Hubby is usually still asleep on the couch. The last half-hour of the family evening is spent in my bed with one or both of the girls, chatting, reading together, or playing fantasy with their stuffed animals. The latter activity with stuffed animals has almost dwindled into childhood oblivion, and I am thrilled when it is resurrected for an evening. We talk about everything, such as their friends at school, vacation plans, worries, periods, sex—you name it. The cats compete for bed space and always lose. At 9:00, we wake their father up for tuck-in and prayers; he generally goes back downstairs to watch sports, and I go back to bed with my own book. Many nights I can hear the girls talking in whispers between their twin beds, and I like this sound.

I am often asleep before they are.

Appendix A

Resources

CAREGIVERS' SUPPORT RESOURCES

- *AgingCare.com:* AgingCare.com helps people caring for elderly parents to find support, resources and information, and a place to connect with other caregivers. Contact: 1-239-594-3235; http://www.agingcare.com
- *Caregiver.com:* This website is operated by the Caregiver Media Group, which produces *Today's Caregiver*, the first national magazine dedicated to caregivers. Contact: 1-800-829-2734; http://www.caregiver.com
- *Centers for Medicare and Medicaid Services (CMS):* CMS helps family caregivers access and use valuable health care information, services, and resources. Contact: http://www.medicare.gov/caregivers
- *Children of Aging Parents (CAPS):* CAPS assists caregivers of the aging with information and referrals, support groups, and programs. Contact: 1-800-227-7294; http://www.caps4caregivers.org
- *Disability.gov:* This federal government website provides easy access to disability-related information and resources. Contact: http://www.disability.gov/
- *Eldercare Locator:* Eldercare Locator provides referrals to area agencies on aging via zip code. Contact: 1-800-677-1116; http://www.eldercare.gov
- *Home Instead:* The Home Instead website offers advice on how to talk to aging parents about difficult issues. Contact: http://www.4070talk.com
- *HospiceDirectory.org:* A list of hospices throughout North America is available at no cost through this online consumer database. Information

regarding hospices and end-of-life care is provided. Contact: 1-800-868-5171; http://hospicedirectory.org/

- *National Alliance for Caregiving (NAC):* The NAC is a nonprofit coalition of national organizations focusing on issues of family caregiving. Contact: 1-800-896-3650; http://www.caregiving.org/

- *National Family Caregivers Association:* This association provides a wealth of resources for the caregiver, including information regarding local resources, caregiving organizations, and advocacy and support resources. Contact: http://www.thefamilycaregiver.org/caregiving_resources/agencies_and_organizations.cfm

- *National Family Caregiver Support Program:* This program assists family and informal caregivers in caring for loved ones at home for as long as possible. Its range of services includes information for caregivers about available services, assistance to caregivers in gaining access to services, individual counseling, organization of support groups, caregiver training, and respite care supplemental services on a limited basis. Contact: 1-202-357-0724; Eldercare Locator (to find local resources): 800-677-1116; http://www.eldercare.gov

- *Medicare.gov:* This website provides a complete caregiver resource list, including tips, facts, checklists, state resources, publications, financial assistance resources, and other federal resources for caregiving. Contact: http://www.medicare.gov/caregivers

- *Rural Caregiver:* Rural Caregiver focuses on specific information and support for rural caregivers. Contact: http://caregiver.com/channels/rural/index.htm

- *ShareTheCaregiving—also known as Share the Care:* This grassroots organization is dedicated to preventing caregiver burnout by promoting and educating people about using the Share the Care model, based on group caregiving. Contact: 1-212-991-9688; http://www.sharethecare.org

- *U.S. Administration on Aging:* This is the official federal agency dedicated to the delivery of supportive home- and community-based services to older individuals and their caregivers. Contact: 1-202-619-0724; http://www.aoa.gov

FINANCIAL HELP RESOURCES

- *Medicare Rights Center:* This center provides hotlines to direct services, education/training, policy briefs, and a list of discount drug programs. Its website includes a list of phone numbers for each state's health insurance assistance programs and information on the new Medicare law for prescription drug cards. Contact: 1460 Broadway, 11th Floor, New York, NY 10036; 1-888-HMO-9050; http://www.medicarerights.org

- *Medicine Program:* The Medicine Program is for those who have no coverage through insurance or government subsidies for outpatient prescription drugs and who cannot afford to purchase medications at retail prices. Contact: P.O. Box 515, Doniphan, MO 63935; 1-573-996-7300; http://www.themedicineprogram.com

- *Partnership for Prescription Assistance (PPA):* The PPA website, operated by the Pharmaceutical Manufacturers Association, has information related to companies' discounts and free programs. Contact: http://www.pparx.org/

- *Together Rx Access:* A free prescription savings card is available for eligible residents of the United States and Puerto Rico who have no prescription drug coverage; the Together Rx Access website includes information on Medicare Part D. Contact: 1-800-444-4106; http://www.togetherrxaccess.com

- *U.S. Department of Health and Human Services, National Clearinghouse for Long-Term Care Information:* The clearinghouse provides information on planning and financing long-term care, including planning for end-of-life care and all major types of public and private financing to help cover long-term care costs. Contact: http://www.longtermcare.gov; email: info@agis.com

RESPITE CARE RESOURCES

- *Easter Seals:* Easter Seals provides a variety of services at 400 sites nationwide for children and adults with disabilities, including adult day care and in-home care. Contact: 1-800-221-6827; http://www.easter-seals.org

- *National Respite Coalition (NRC):* The NRC provides a list of states that have respite coalitions. Contact: 1-703-256-9578; http://www.archrespite.org

- *Shepherd's Centers of America:* This organization provides respite care, telephone visits, in-home visits, nursing home visits, home health aides, adult day care, and information and referrals. Contact: http://shepherdcenters.org; email: staff@shepherdcenters.org

- Meals on Wheels

PARENTING RESOURCES

- *The Compassionate Friends:* This group offers telephone support and understanding to families who have lost a child; it provides a resource library and newsletter. Contact: 1-877-969-0010; http://www .compassionatefriends.org
- *Family Voices:* Family Voices offers information on health care policies relevant to special needs children in every state. Contact: 1-888-835 -5669; http://www.familyvoices.org

DISEASE-SPECIFIC AND HEALTH-RELATED AGENCIES AND WEBSITES

This list is provided by the National Health Council: http://nhcouncil .org

- Alzheimer's Association: 1-800-272-3900; http://www.alz.org
- American Autoimmune Related Disease Association: 1-800-598-4668; http://www.aarda.org
- American Cancer Society: 1-800-ACS-2345; http://www.cancer.org
- American Diabetes Association: 1-800-342-2383; http://www.diabetes.org
- American Foundation for AIDS Research: 1-800-392-6327; http://amfar .org
- American Heart Association: 1-800-AHA-USA-1; www.heart.org/ HEARTORG

Appendix B

The Caregiver's Creed

I HAVE CHOICE.

I can choose to take this day and be grateful for it, or I can choose to be miserable. My life is in my own hands. I will choose to notice my thoughts when they are negative and consciously change them to more positive ways of thinking. I will remember that I am in charge of my own life and emotions. I will remind myself that, if I make my negative thinking more positive, my behaviors will naturally shift to more loving ones, and I will feel less resentful.

I WILL PUT MYSELF FIRST.

I will not be able to care for others if I am physically or emotionally drained. I must recognize that I must put myself first. If I can do this, I will be much better equipped to love, care for, and support my family. I will allow myself to feel all my feelings, including guilt. I will notice the feelings and then still do what I need to do to take care of myself. I may feel an emotion such as guilt, but I do not need to let it rule how I function.

I WILL TAKE TIME FOR MYSELF AND MY PARTNER.

 I can and will take time each day for myself and also for my partner. If the telephone rings and I see it is someone I want to talk to who will listen to *me*, I will pick up the phone. When I need a break, I will have an established break room or place and inform my family that I will be resting for a half-hour. I will remember to look up at the sky. I will buy myself a small gift. I will paint my toes. I will have a night out each week, and I will maintain exercise or a hobby that pleases me.

I will also remember to make time for my partner and let him know how important he is to me. I will do small things each day to show him I love him. I will write him a note, or send him a text message, or have a quiet cup of coffee with him. I will remember to acknowledge his presence and love.

I WILL ESTABLISH A ROUTINE.

 This will decrease chaos and increase my feelings of mastery of my environment. I will know much of what I can expect during the day, who will do it, and when it will get done. This will help the whole family know when I am available or not, so I can feel less guilty.

I WILL ASK FOR HELP.

I will ask a loved one or friend for help/respite, and/or I will hire help, so I will get a break and not be so isolated or alone. I will call family meetings to ensure that everyone in the family pitches in, and I will teach my children to help their grandparents.

I CAN SAY YES, MAYBE, LATER, OR NO.

It is my job to protect myself. I will have many things that I am required to do; however, I will also have many opportunities to set boundaries. When I make the decision to do something, I will be as positive as I can because it was my decision and choice. I will practice saying no, setting limits, and protecting my own time.

I WILL PAY ATTENTION TO MY OWN FEELINGS AND NEEDS.
I will notice if I am beginning to feel overwhelmed and set a boundary before it gets out of hand. I will notice when I feel guilty and still do what I need to do to take care of myself. Feelings just *are*. I can notice my feelings and still move forward without getting pulled back into old traps. If my feelings become unmanageable and I feel out of control, I can get professional help.

I WILL REMIND MYSELF THAT THIS IS MY ONE LIFE TO LIVE.
When I need a reason to do something for myself, I will consciously remind myself that this is *my* life; it is not my parents' or my children's life, and I must be responsible for making myself happy. No one else can be in charge of my happiness.

Notes

CHAPTER ONE

1. Arnold H. Modell, *Object Relations Theory: Psychic Aliveness in the Middle Years* (New Haven, CT: Yale University Press, 1989).
2. Erik Erikson, *Childhood and Society* (New York: W. W. Norton, 1950).
3. Ibid.
4. Merriam-Webster Dictionary, http://www.merriam-webster.com/dictionary/sandwich+generation
5. Charles R. Pierret, "The Sandwich Generation: Women Caring for Parents and Children" (*Monthly Labor Review*, September 2006).
6. Ibid.

CHAPTER TWO

1. Florine Livson, *Paths to Psychological Health in the Middle Years* (New York: Academic, 1981).
2. Kristine Bertini, *Marital Status and Midlife* (Ann Arbor: University of Michigan Press, 1995).
3. Elaine Wethington, "Americans and the 'Midlife Crisis' " (*Motivation and Emotion*, 24(2): 85–103, 2000).
4. Carlo Strenger, "Paring Down Life to the Essentials" (*Psychoanalytic Psychology*, 26(3): 246–258, 2009).
5. Ernest Becker, *The Denial of Death* (New York: Free Press, 1974).
6. Erik Erikson, *Childhood and Society* (New York: W. W. Norton, 1950).

7. Centers for Disease Control and Prevention, Chronic Disease Prevention and Health Promotion, http://www.cdc.gov/nccdphp (modified 2009).

8. *Sexuality in Midlife and Beyond* (AARP, 2007).

9. Institute on Aging, *Midlife in the U.S. (MIDUS)* (Madison: University of Wisconsin, 2002).

10. Kristine Bertini, *Understanding and Preventing Suicide* (Westport, CT: Praeger, 2009).

11. Merriam-Webster Online Dictionary, http://www.merriam-webster .com.

12. Erik Erikson, *Childhood and Society* (New York: W. W. Norton, 1950).

13. Kristine Bertini, *Understanding and Preventing Suicide* (Westport, CT: Praeger, 2009).

14. Carl Jung, *The Development of the Personality: The Collected Works of C. J. Jung* (New York: Pantheon Books, 1925), vol. 17, pp. 187–201.

15. Daniel Levinson, *The Seasons of a Woman's Life* (New York: Knopf, 1996).

16. Henri Bergson, *Time and Free Will* (New York: Macmillan, 1889).

17. Alfred Adler, *Understanding Human Nature* (New York: Greenberg, 1927).

18. Janet Landman, Elizabeth Vandewater, Abagail Stewart, & Janet Malley, "Missed Opportunities: Psychological Ramifications of Counterfactual Thought in Midlife Women" (*Journal of Adult Development*, 2: 87–97, 1995).

19. Carlo Strenger & Arie Ruttenberg, "The Existential Necessity of Midlife Change" (*Harvard Business Review*, 82–90, February 2008).

CHAPTER THREE

1. Donald Winnicott, *The Motivational Processes and the Facilitating Environment: Studies in the Theory of Emotional Development* (New York: International Universities Press, 1974).

2. Mireille Joussemet et al., "A Self-Determination Perspective on Parenting" (*Canadian Psychology*, 49(3): 194–200, 2008).

3. Tetyana Pudrovska, "Psychological Implications of Motherhood and Fatherhood in Midlife: Evidence from Sibling Models" (*Journal of Marriage and Family*, 70: 168–181, February 2008).

4. Ibid.

5. Mirjam N. Stolk et al., *Early Parenting Intervention: Family Risk and First-Time Parenting Related to Intervention Effectiveness* (Luden, Netherland: Springer Science and Business Media, 2007).

6. Karen Coburn & Madge Treeger, *Letting Go: A Parent's Guide to Understanding the College Years* (New York: HarperCollins, 2003).

7. Carlos Valiente et al., "Children's Responses to Daily Social Stressors: Relations with Parenting, Children's Effortful Control, and Adjustment" (*Journal of Child Psychology and Psychiatry*, 50(6): 707–717, 2009).

8. Ibid.

9. Jonathan Murray & David Murray, *Two for the Money: Financial Success for the Sandwich Generation* (New York: Carroll & Graf, 2006).

10. *Kiplinger's Financial Solutions for the Sandwich Generation* (Chicago: Kaplan Business, 2006).

CHAPTER FOUR

1. Brent Mallinckrodt, "Childhood Emotional Bonds with Parents, Development of Adult Social Competencies, and Availability of Social Support" (*Journal of Counseling Psychology*, 39(4): 453–461, 1992).

2. Ibid.

3. Abraham Maslow, *Motivation and Personality* (New York: Harper & Row, 1954).

4. John Bowlby, *Attachment and Loss* (New York: Basic Books, 1999).

5. Michael Henderson, *Forgiveness: Breaking the Chain of Hate* (Portland, OR: Arnica, 2003).

6. Huston Smith, *The World's Religions* (New York: HarperCollins, 1991).

7. Janet Clark & Katherine Weber, *Challenges and Choices: Elderly Caregiving* (University of Missouri Extension Publications (extension. missouri.edu/pub), 1997).

CHAPTER FIVE

1. Janet Clark & Katherine Weber, *Challenges and Choices: Elderly Caregiving* (Missouri extension publications, University of Missouri Extension [extension.missouri.edu/pub], 1997).

CHAPTER SIX

1. Dave Ramsey, "Sandwich Generation" in Financial Bind, http://www.cbsnews.com/stories/2007/08/07/earlyshow/contributors/daveramsey/main3140482.shtml (2007).

2. Ibid.

3. Karen McCormack, *Strategies for the "Sandwich Generation"* (Business Week Investing Survival Guide, Oct 16, 2007, http://www.businessweek.com/investing/special_reports/20061016investingsu.htm).

4. Ibid.

5. Ameriprise Financial, *Money across Generations: The Sandwich Generation, Planning for Family Needs While Keeping Your Financial Goals on Track* (July 2007), http://www.ameriprise.com/global/docs/pr-money-generations-research.pdf.

6. Ibid.

7. Ibid.

8. Rande Spiegelman, *Solutions for the Sandwich Generation* (Schwab Center for Financial Research, 2008), http://www.schwab.com/public/schwab/research_strategies/market_insight/financial_goals/financial_planning/solutions_for_the_sandwich_generation.html?cmsid=P-1255231&lvl1=research_strategies&lvl2=market_insight.

9. Ibid.

CHAPTER SEVEN

1. Merriam-Webster's Online Dictionary, www.Merriam-Webster.com. 11th ed. (Springfield, MA: Merriam-Webster, 2007).

2. Donald Winnicott, *The Motivational Process and the Facilitating Environment: Studies in the Theory of Emotional Development* (New York: International Universities Press, 1974).

3. John Bowlby, *Attachment and Loss* (New York: Basic Books, 1999).

4. Stephen Covey & David Hatch, *Everyday Greatness* (TN: Thomas Nelson, 2006).

Index

About the Author

Dr. Kristine Bertini is a clinical psychologist and Director of Health and Counseling Services at the University of Southern Maine. She is a returned Peace Corps volunteer from the country of Micronesia and remains in close contact with her extended local family there. She volunteers with the American Red Cross. Dr. Bertini lives in Maine with her husband, stepdaughters, elderly parents, and herd of cats.